THE STADIUM

Architecture for the New Global Culture

Rod Sheard

Text
Rod Sheard
Robert Powell
Patrick Bingham-Hall

Photography
Patrick Bingham-Hall

PERIPLUS

Published by Periplus Editions with editorial offices at
130 Joo Seng Road #06-01/03 Singapore 368357
by arrangement with Pesaro Publishing, Sydney, Australia.

Editor: Patrick Bingham-Hall
Design: Mark Thacker
Photography © Patrick Bingham-Hall except
where otherwise credited.
Text © Pesaro Publishing and authors

ISBN 0-7946-0335-1

Distributed by
North America, Latin America & Europe
Tuttle Publishing
364 Innovation Drive
North Clarendon, VT 05759-9436
Tel: (802) 773 8930
Fax: (802) 773 6993
Email: info@tuttlepublishing.com
www.tuttlepublishing.com

Japan
Tuttle Publishing
Yaekari Building, 3F
5-4-12 Osaki, Shinagawu-ku
Tokyo 141-0032
Tel: (03) 5437 0171
Fax: (03) 5437 0755
Email: tuttle-sales@gol.com

Asia Pacific
Berkeley Books Pte Ltd
130 Joo Seng Road, #06-01/03
Singapore 368357
Tel: (65) 6280 1330
Fax; (65) 6280 6290
Email: inquiries@periplus.com.sg
www.periplus.com

10 09 08 07 06 05
5 4 3 2 1

Printed in Singapore

"Where the crowds gather history is made."

Spiro Kostov

Spiro Kostov The City Assembled; The Elements of Urban Form through History. *Thames and Hudson, London, 1992.*

"A stadium, more than any other building type in history, has the ability to shape a town or city. A stadium is able to put a community on the map, establishing an identity and providing a focal point in the landscape.

Stadia are the most 'viewed' buildings in history and have the power to change people's lives: they represent a nation's pride and aspirations. They can be massively expensive to build, but they can also generate huge amounts of money. The power and fiscal weight of sport is increasing as an industry around the world, and I believe the 21st Century will establish sport as the world's first truly global culture. It will become the internationally recognised social currency.

Consequently the stadium will become the most important building any community can own, and if it is used wisely, it will be the most useful urban planning tool a city can possess. In the last 150 years, since sport was codified and professionalised, there has been a dramatic shift to urbanisation, from the country to the city, and the meteoric rise in the popularity of sport has been the consequence..."

Rod Sheard

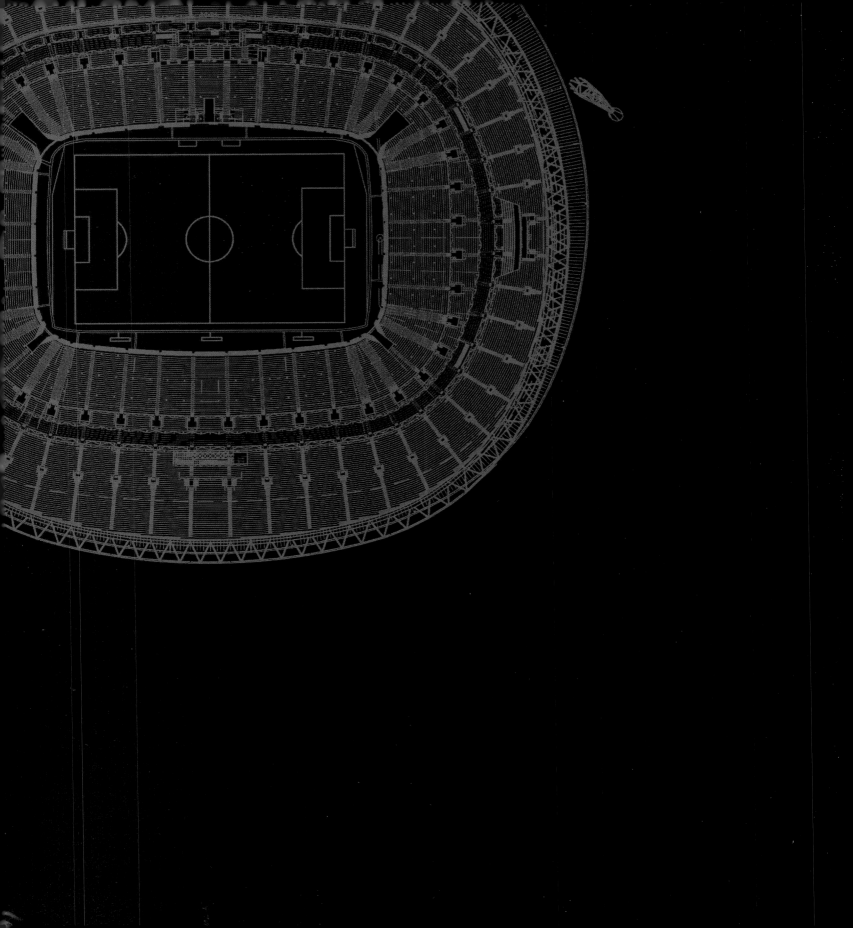

Contents

Rome of the Carolinas

SITTING THERE IN ROME – and not just a craggy old monument – the Colosseum still oozes action and power. Its form races round in space with that tricky – but tempting – ability to grab a 'dynamic' and transmit a sense of that grabbing over the two thousand years of its existence.

We don't just need to be prompted by Technicolor blockbusters with surround sound to remind us of what went on, because it's surely there in the stone and the serried arches that swish past us. The body of the building is, of course, the massive construct that held all those screaming onlookers. Its soul: the now silent field. No plaza, no stage, no altar, no dais – can approach its aura of dramatic expectation. Yet the architecture is direct, the geometry is obvious, and the architectural rhetoric (despite all this heroism) is remarkably well under control.

The Pantheon, by contrast, has to resort to devices – its magic eye is brilliantly cunning, of course, but nonetheless it is a contrivance.

So there, in a nutshell, is the basic challenge of architecture. How to deftly capture magic? Especially when dealing with the challenge of the Event: the Game and the assembly are theatre. The body can somehow celebrate the sense of expectation – at every stage from turnstile, cloakroom, bar, television room, players' tunnel, and even more so when these things intertwine and feed each other. Put a body of people queuing, hustling and rustling, and you have something infinitely more electric than a town of similar size to that crowd.

Think of it, even an average sized 2nd division grandstand will hold the equivalent of a serious dot on a map. Then ignite the game or the event – and you generate a take-off of greater dynamic than that of a wide-bodied jet on the runway.

Since we've introduced the subject of airports, they are (if anything), the other modern equivalent of the traditional town: where a town-sized body of people are gathered together, involved in a continuous series of 'surges' and expectations and where the architecture gains by recognising this and nurturing it. However, in both cases, other motivations are fighting their way into the conversation.

"You've got all those people there captive" goes one argument, "now find them more things to do, to buy, or to incorporate into the afternoon out or the trip. With another argument in parallel, "You've got all that building stacked up there and when the game's over or the planes have left: why, it's all just SITTING there for God's sake! What can we DO with it?

Some years ago I found myself in the campus town of Norman, Oklahoma (as one does). I had come to give a lecture at the architecture school of the University (...no ordinary school, by the way, as it was the Domain of a certain Professor Bruce Goff – one of the nuttiest and most original architects of the Old West, along with his priceless library of European tomes). On enquiry, I was directed towards the enormous football stadium. Wait a minute... Could this be right? I asked again, but it was surely not a joke – all this intellectual energy, all this wonderfully arcane stuff (and the three hundred students that indulged in it) were to be found strung along under rows 'D' to 'XX' on the south side of the stadium.

What a great idea!

One speculates: did Goff's voice soar above the echoes of the field? Did the ambition of the students rise with the progressive rumble of an expectant crowd? In other words, does a sports building have to limit itself to a narrow set of consistencies? Or does this unlikely case hint at new initiative and more imagination in the creation of a 'place'? Did the presence of the architecture studios not add some piquancy to the situation? A bit of mystery? Couldn't this type of thing go further? Imagine the whole underside of stadium terraces infested with a myriad of activities. The frozen town acting as host to an unfrozen town. Or, to (once again) reverse the proposition: let the town enliven itself by acting host to the event space. The medieval London Bridge had houses straddling it, and of course, in the great scheme of things, the bridge was the key item. But those houses.... why, they cheered it up on a cold night: they were parasites and they celebrated their good luck at being there.

Another vagabond's memory, this time from South Carolina: after an hour's drive from the airport, through lush and well-tempered countryside, there was a sudden vision. Like Bluebeard's castle on acid, an enormous, beautiful thing loomed up out of the trees: not apparently surrounded by anything in particular. This, the stadium of Clemson (and its University which was there, somewhere under the trees) seemed to come out of a fairytale. It had class, it had guts and it certainly had presence, though oddly enough, I don't remember much about the architecture except, like the team, it felt GREAT.

So we have the stadium as point of arrival, as point of focus, and in terms of urban theory: the point of departure. From a well-honed, well-sited, and (I would suggest) a well-infested event structure we can conjure up a wonderful 'town' of the 21st century.

In our day-to-day survival, we have moved into the world of the hybrid. We live in the reality of the folded-over experience, with fun-and-games as seriousness: one activity as a trigger for other activities, with a crowd rumbling through the turnstiles with a variety of needs or indulgences to be tapped. The best and most ingenious architects are celebrating and articulating the magic of the event – with a giant arch or a sweeping curve; a slithering, moving canopy; a preying, gesticulating gangway or a striding leg or two on the go. Yet simultaneously they are beginning to incorporate witty combinations of activity; some circumstantial, some entrepreneurial and many 'inspired'.

We are at an interesting moment in history, for we have a combination of high technology and a multiplicity of creative know-how. We have a cultural accumulation ready to be to be raided. From the best resources of anthropological observation, economic ingenuity, sense of theatre, even creative cynicism (if you wish): we can now make the Colosseum to be Rome or Rome to be the Colosseum.

PETER COOK

11

Sport is the new Rock'n'Roll[1]

Something happened, and it happened in the early 1990s: the ascendancy of sport.

The ascendancy of sport coincided with and resulted from a number of demographic stops and starts, and one seismic shift occurred as the Baby Boomers hit middle age and became passive cultural identities: their interests (and occasional creative outbursts) gradually switched to nostalgia. The cultural language of the 1960s had been rock'n'roll, and although its revolutionary idealism died out at the end of the decade (officially at the Altamont Speedway on December 6, 1969), rock'n'roll remained the globally dominant popular entertainment for another twenty years. But its time in the sun had passed.

Above: Reliant Stadium – Houston, Texas, USA 2002

John Berger's musings on the Cubist movement (which began in 1907) are relevant – "Cubism should be considered not as a stylistic category but as a moment (even if a moment lasting six or seven years) experienced by a certain number of people. A strangely placed moment. It was a moment in which the promises of the future were more substantial than the present".[2] And so it was with the glory days of rock'n'roll, but the business of rock'n'roll lived on, it was far too popular to die. It became mass entertainment, controlled by the 'music industry', and the glory days were not shelved as a precious artistic moment.[3] But rock'n'roll was in creative decline, and it was eclipsed by a more universally relevant form of mass entertainment. The biggest stars of rock'n'roll were the biggest stars of postwar society – Elvis, the Beatles, Michael Jackson and Madonna – but they were not succeeded as superstars by other musical performers. The biggest stars of the last ten years have been sportsmen – Michael Jordan, Diego Maradona, Sachin Tendulkar and Tiger Woods.

It could be suggested that there are three fundamental reasons for the ascendancy of sport: satellite television, the digital revolution and the 'worldwide web'; the globalization of the world economy; and sport's unique capacity to reinvent itself.

"United's victory in the first ever Premiership [1993] meant the club was perfectly poised to take advantage of the new money being thrown at the game. With Sky TV and its cheerleaders in the popular press shouting the game up constantly, football became the new version of Hollywood......United found themselves sitting on a mint".[4]

Television transformed sport in the 1990s with the amounts of money generated globally by cable and satellite networks, and sport did become the new rock'n'roll, or the new Hollywood. The groundwork had been laid by (mainly American) television broadcasters and entrepreneurs, most notably Ted Turner who, in the 1970s, "was prescient enough to anticipate that the future of sport lay in the hands of television".[5] A turning point was the acceptance (within the sports) of professionalism. Many sports, notably tennis, cricket, athletics and rugby union made the occasionally painful switch from a noble unpaid amateur tradition to a full-time professional business. Although this did not automatically increase the popularity of the sports, it inevitably led to a co-existence between sport and the mass media. The sportsmen (and women) had to be paid by somebody, and the simplest, most obvious, method was to establish a large spectator base. And television was the way. The subsequent phenomenon of cross-ownership (or multi-media) arose whereby corporations operated a variety of media types within their organization – cable television, free to air television, radio, magazines, internet, advertising and merchandising. Perhaps the most brazen, and unexpected, manoeuvre was the acquisition of a financial interest (often a controlling interest) in sporting teams by a media organization. The names of the media 'moguls' are now, most appropriately, part of sporting legend – Ted Turner, Kerry Packer, Silvio Berlusconi and Rupert Murdoch. The latter's name is even honoured by the academic appellation of 'Murdochization', which "refers to a process by which corporations primarily involved in the mass media of communications appropriate and integrate into their organizations sports clubs". [6]

With the decline of interest in rock'n'roll (and, less conspicuously, in other forms of popular entertainment) sport was gold-plated. It appealed just as much as it ever had to teenagers, and the generations following the Baby Boomers had been excluded from the glory days of rock'n'roll and the rosy glow of the Swinging Sixties. And, crucially, sport now appealed more than ever to 'emerging' nations, by which we mean nations who were now making serious money and could afford to support sport, whether played in their own country or vicariously via television. This circumstance can loosely be explained as globalization, both economic and cultural. One claim is that this has created an American cultural hegemony. In 1992, Todd Gitlin wrote in the New York Times that "American popular culture is the closest approximation there is today to a global lingua franca".[7] And in 2004, again in the New York Times, Alan Riding suggested that "As Europe moves toward 'ever closer

1 The phrase is adapted from Ellis Cashmore, Sports Culture: An A-Z Guide, Routledge, London, 2000, p ix. Ellis Cashmore wrote "Sport is now a form of entertainment, what some writers call the new rock'n'roll".
2 John Berger, Selected Essays, Edited by Geoff Dyer, Pantheon, 2000.
3 Cubism is described as "the most extraordinary artistic movement of the century" in Larousse Encyclopedia of Modern Art, Hamlyn Publishing Group, 1980.
4 Jim White and Andy Mitten, A Rough Guide to Man Utd 2003-2004 Season, Rough Guides Ltd, London, 2003, p 376.

5 Ellis Cashmore, Sports Culture: An A–Z Guide, p 423
6 ibid: Page 292
7 Todd Gitlin "World leaders: Mickey et al", New York Times, May 3, 1992.

union', unless it also communicates culturally, popular taste will become ever more American".[8] It would appear though, that the reverse has occurred in sport. The ascendancy of sport has been marked by the undeniable global dominance of soccer, 'the world game', which is manifestly not an American game. Cricket (possibly the second most popular 'world game', certainly for spectators) also has a peripheral presence in the USA. Soccer, cricket and rugby union have tremendously successful World Cups every four years, and the USA (usually) has no more than a cameo role.[9] The dominant American games of baseball, basketball, (American) football and ice hockey are dabbled with by other nations, but they hardly constitute a lingua franca.

A serious and traditional form of architecture[10]

The landmarks and the symbols of our cities and our cultures have been the built monuments. For better or for worse, they show what we were and what we are. That many of the monuments (Schloss Neuschwanstein, the Taj Mahal) were follies could be an honest assessment of human achievement. But the monumental structures mark our civilization(s), and the architecture of the great cities endures as our most popular art-form. It could hardly be otherwise, it is there for us all to see.

There has been a rush, a rash, of monument building since the

Sport itself has become a lingua franca. We know how – money, television and global communication – but why has it happened? Sport has always been popular for basic reasons – mankind's innate competitive rituals, the need or desire for physical activity, a tribal passion expressed as national or civic pride and (more mundanely) a distraction from a workaday world. But sport has attained an undeniable position as the new global culture, and this recent phenomenon may simply be due to sport's inherent capacity to reinvent and restage itself. Every sporting event, one trusts, is unpredictable and unscripted.

This does not apply so comprehensively to other forms of mass entertainment. If you watch the Rolling Stones in concert, or the Three Tenors, or attend a performance of Romeo and Juliet, you have a fair idea of what's going to happen and you (probably) won't be surprised. But if you go to a baseball game or cricket match, you may be able to pick the winner in advance, but that's about it. And you'll probably get that wrong. Sport exists as a continuum within our society, which gradually reinforces its attraction with each new generation. The current star players are perceived as the peers of previous legendary players. In baseball, Barry Bonds follows on from Joe Dimaggio and Babe Ruth; in soccer, Zidane follows Platini and di Stefano; in tennis, Serena Williams follows Martina Navratilova and Billie Jean King. And so on. Sport's role in popular culture is gold-plated, it will require a cultural or spiritual shift, rather than a generational change, to alter that.

1960s. An 'icon' is required by every city. If the city is 'icon-free', it's a loser. 'Icon building' is now a worldwide competition - the 'Olympic Games of Global Citydom'. It would seem that this modern version of an ancient sport began with the Sydney Opera House, which catapulted Sydney instantly into 'World City' status and removed her local rivals from competition. The Sydney Opera House launched a million postcards and firework displays. It made Sydney and Australia famous, and the local economy laughed all the way to the bank. An irony, nay an anachronism, should be observed here. An adolescent, rough around the edges and egalitarian nation realized fame and fortune through that most rarefied and elitist of indulgences – opera. All power to the 'icon'.

So pick an adolescent city or a rundown rust-belt city, and the Sydney Opera House principle will have been applied at sometime in the last thirty years. Now it is often referred to as the

8 Alan Riding, "A not so united bunch when it comes to creativity", *New York Times*.
9 It must be noted that the USA reached the quarter finals of the 2002 Soccer World Cup, and were generally adjudged as one of the most skilful teams in the tournament. The USA Women's soccer team have carried all before them in recent times, and took the gold medal at the 2004 Olympic Games.
10 This phrase is adapted from 'The writing of the walls: Architecture as propaganda' by Alain de Botton, published in the International Herald Tribune, July 13 2004. De Botton actually wrote "To

defend many works of recent architecture, one could therefore argue that they are rather nobly trying to change the way we perceive certain places and cities and forms of travel......Even if we don't always approve of their appearance, we should at least be sympathetic to the ambitions behind their constructions. They represent attempts to lend dignity to their surroundings, and that – assuming the ceiling doesn't cave in – may be one of the most serious and traditional functions of architecture".

Above: Melbourne Cricket Ground Redevelopment – Melbourne, Australia
2006 (scheduled completion)

Melbourne Cricket Ground was designed by the MCG5 Architects; a joint venture between HOK
Sport + Venue + Event, TS+E, Hassell, The Cox Group and Daryl Jackson Pty Ltd.

Bilbao principle, in honour of Frank Gehry's Guggenheim Museum, completed in 1997. The city of Bilbao in northern Spain, previously a rust-belt casualty, is now back on the world map. Many great cities, of course, have little need for 'icon building', but most of them do it anyway. Paris, Beijing, New York and Rome would appear to have no room for further postcard opportunities, but the game continues: Global City rankings are continually updated.

And these modern monuments? These global 'icons'? These instant Opera Houses? ..... what building type has been preferred as the symbol of a city?

It is tempting to believe that in some cases, the building's function has been irrelevant, other than that of icon. Although, as Alain de Botton observes[11] "..to imply that this strays from architecture's historical goals is to deny history".

The architectural magazines would have us believe that the recent 'icons' have been museums, art galleries, libraries and airports. Which are rather odd building types for a monument at the end of the 20th Century. Is a museum or a library symbolic of our time - the computer age? Probably not. The architecture itself most certainly is, nobody can deny the zeitgeist of a swerving titanium-clad computer-modeled Gehry museum, but there is a continuation of the Sydney Opera House irony – the appropriation of an elitist, vaguely anachronistic, function for a building that will (hopefully) reinvent a city. Airports are unquestionably symbols of our times, but whether they exist as prestige buildings, outside the pages of architectural magazines, is a moot point. Airports are of drudge, the sounds of shuffling feet and tired suitcases. And of post 9-11 paranoia.

Spiritual aspirations have explained monument construction since Imhotep first designed a pyramid (in Saqqara c.2760 BC). The ancient monuments were officially tombs and temples, but the (monumental) ruins of more prosaic structures endure –

Left: Estádio Algarve – Faro/Loulé, Algarve, Portugal 2004

11 ibid

aqueducts, bathing halls, outdoor theatres and, most notably, the amphitheatres. The Colosseum has quite a legacy. The monumental structures of mediaeval Europe were the Gothic cathedrals, and with their surrounding squares (or piazze) they were, and generally still are, the civic and cultural hearts of their cities. Monumental secular architecture crept back during the Renaissance, reaching its apogee with the construction of Versailles, but the true precedents for our 21st Century Global City 'icons' were the cathedrals of Europe and the mosques of Islam. These buildings strove for glory (ostensibly spiritual) but also for status (economic, political) for their cities - Florence, Siena, Constantinople, Cairo, Prague, Seville. Apart from supplying a formal civic focus, the cathedral and its square also provided a communal space, often for massive crowds. The *palio* horse races in the Piazza del Campo, in the centre of Siena, are a chaotic reminder of life in a 14th Century city-state, an early Global City.

Modern monuments, symbols of a secular age, appeared in the 19th Century. The French Revolution and the American War of Independence inspired an egalitarian optimism and the real possibility of a new world. And the Industrial Revolution supplied the technology. The heroic iron structures of the railway stations and exhibition buildings in London, Paris and New York transformed the image of these cities. They were dramatic (and romantic) symbols of those great cities. And great cities they were, on a scale that had never been seen before. London's population grew from less than 2 million in 1800 to 6.5 million in 1900 – it was the largest city in history. The Crystal Palace, St Pancras Station, the Albert Memorial and the Houses of Parliament were monuments to this new metropolis. But the artistic spirit of the 19th Century belonged to Paris, and her architectural monuments extend from L'Arc de Triomphe through the Bibliotheque Nationale, the Opera, the Gare du Nord and Gare de L'Est to the triumphant Eiffel Tower.

It was New York, of course, which ushered in the quintessential city building type, the 'icon' for the Modern age – the skyscraper. The skyscraper is still utilized, individually or collectively – en masse as a cityscape – as the image for a new or reinvented city. The putative emerging cities of Asia are festooned and forested with them – Hong Kong, Singapore, Dubai, Kuala Lumpur, Taipei, Shenzhen, Beijing and, most spectacularly, Shanghai. But in the Old World, for a variety of reasons, the skyscraper is no longer the 'instant icon'. It would appear that recent skyscrapers in Europe and the USA are regarded as generic at best, and rather tired and tiresome at worst. Or, quite simply, social values may have changed and there is no longer an immutable respect for the symbol of the 'greed is good' culture.

A building type which neatly sidesteps the incongruities and ironies of 21st Century 'icons' is the stadium. The ascendancy of sport as the new global culture means that a stadium has a central role (position) in the city – financial, political, geographical and spiritual.

The Lonely Planet Guide to Beijing refers to the city's preparation for the 2008 Olympic Games as "the Holy Grail of Beijing city planners".[12] As stadia are fundamentally buildings for (happy) people, they are just as likely to be remembered for the events which occurred within them as for their design, so there is a reciprocal public relations arrangement between the architecture of the stadium and its function. And, of course, there is a similar reciprocal arrangement between the stadium (and event) and the host city. For all the bright cardinal-red exuberance of the Estádio da Luz in Lisbon, the venue is currently renowned for two wayward penalty kicks by David Beckham. Reliant Stadium in Houston hosted the 2004 Super Bowl... and, most memorably, Janet Jackson's wardrobe malfunction.

The greatest buildings, the 'icons', have always reflected the zeitgeist. And right now, the zeitgeist is sport: it is the global currency.

12 Damian Harper, Beijing, Lonely Planet Publications, Melbourne, 2002

Opposite: The arch for the new Wembley Stadium is winched into place, June 2004. The massive arch is 350 metres wide and 135 metres tall, and it will support the world's largest single span roof.

"The scene was set – a rare sunny day in Cardiff, the finest venue in the United Kingdom and a match between the biggest two clubs in the British Isles".[15]

"I was watching Arsenal play Newcastle United at Highbury last year, from the North Bank Stand. There was a scuffle of some sort in the penalty box, right in front of us, 30 yards away, and Newcastle got a penalty. There was pandemonium all round, but it happened so quick that nobody knew why the penalty had been given. They don't have instant replays on large screens at Highbury. So I rang my daughter at home in Australia who was watching the game live on Fox Sports at 6 in the morning... "Um, yeah Dad, it was a handball." So I told everybody around me, and the word was passed on – "Some Australian geezer rang his daughter in Sydney and she said it was handball". So from a beanbag in Balmain, my 6 year old daughter enlightened the Arsenal faithful".[13]

The fifth dimension has no physical surrounding. It is abstract.

A sporting event is not just experienced by the privileged few who have tickets to the venue, it is shared by millions around the world. And the experience is equally meaningful, whether you are in the 'real' stadium or the 'virtual' stadium. Indeed, the experience may be far more satisfying in the 'virtual' stadium – a world of perfect sightlines and instant replays (and a well-stocked refrigerator). The 21st Century stadium cannot be perceived as a tangible traditional piece of architecture: its role, its function, its reality is far more than that. The Fifth Generation[14] stadium is the 'virtual' stadium.

The physical realities of stadium architecture are influenced as

Above: Millennium Stadium – Cardiff, Wales 1999

13 Patrick Bingham-Hall in conversation with Rod Sheard. Brisbane, August 3, 2004.
14 See Page 100 in this book for an explanation of the generations of stadia.
15 Jim White and Andy Mitten, The Rough Guide to Man Utd 2003/2004 Season, p 103. A review of the 2003 Worthington Cup Final between Manchester United and Liverpool at the Millennium Stadium in Cardiff.
16 Bud Selig, Major League Baseball Commissioner, quoted in the San Francisco Chronicle, 2000

much by the needs of the invisible audience as they are by the crowd at the venue itself. The stadium is the backdrop for television coverage, and it is imperative that the sense of occasion is established for the television audience, connecting with the viewers and placing them at the event. But this can only be successfully achieved by providing a stadium which also satisfies local demands and requirements. No degree of televisual awareness can overcome the deadening vista of empty seats. Stadium design requires an intimate understanding and awareness of 'place' – the social and cultural priorities of the local fanbase, and the importance of sport, or a sporting team, to a city or a neighbourhood.

Many of the stadia featured in this book have been the venues for the most successful sporting events of the last decade; and as stunning as the architecture may be, there are other prerequisites for the creation of a 'perfect' setting for sport. An additional combination of technical and televisual awareness, cultural sensitivity and sporting knowledge transcends the formal architectural value of the stadium. The architects design for atmosphere, creating an environment where the passion and the intensity can inspire a phenomenon equivalent to musical 'harmonics' (the ear's capacity to imagine a sound or tone, which technically does not exist, but is created by other tones). When Cathy Freeman won the 400 metres at the 2000 Olympic Games, when England won the 2003 Rugby World Cup and when Greece won the the Euro 2004 Championships, they were moments that had far greater significance than mere sporting victory. They stirred unprecedented emotion, both for the crowds in the stadia and for who knows how many millions in the 'virtual' global stadia. This could just be attributed to the 'power of sport', but the phenomenon – the emotional moment – does not occur in all stadia, only in the best. The stadium, both 'real' and 'virtual' is a theatre, and a rudimentary (or generic) theatre cannot provide a stage for the greatest performances.

The best stadia, to coin a phrase, 'just get it right'. And as a result of the ascendancy of sport, the best stadia are the true monuments of our time.

"Camden Yards just might be one of the two or three most powerful developments in the history of baseball".[16]

Above: Oriole Park at Camden Yards – Baltimore, Maryland, USA 1992

Wembley Stadium

London, England

2006 (scheduled completion)

"Anyone who went to Wembley Stadium, whether it was for a football game, rugby match or a concert would probably have agreed that it was a disgrace. As a venue for major international sporting events, it was a dated mess that even its status as the home of football couldn't redeem.

Thankfully, the whole shebang was torn down at the end of 2002, despite protests about the fate of the twin towers: so long the symbol of English football. And while the Scots have the glorious Hampden Park, the temporary HQ down south was transplanted to the awesome Millennium Stadium in Cardiff.

'Wembley for an English football fan is Mecca', says Sven-Goran Eriksson. 'It's part and parcel of the history of football here, so it was absolutely the right decision to rebuild it.'

The new Wembley project is expected to be completed in early 2006, in time to host the FA Cup final, and it will be the most advanced stadium in the world, a benchmark for future stadium construction.

The new Wembley will have 90,000 seats, each with more leg-room than even the old Royal Box offered. This will make it one of the largest stadium buildings in the world with a complete circumference of one kilometre. The roof will be partly retractable, allowing the grass to be exposed to natural sunlight and ventilation. With the roof in its retracted position, games can be played with no shadow falling further than the corner flag. The Wembley architects employed astronomers to calculate the position of the sun in May, so they could design the retractable roof to avoid shadows falling on the pitch on the day of the Cup Final.

The centrepiece of the new stadium is the arch. A wonder of modern architecture, the 315 metre long structure will support the roof; eliminating the need for pillars, so the view of the pitch is not obstructed from anywhere within the stadium. The arch, which could fit the London Eye between the top and the pitch, will be a new landmark on the London skyline."

Scot Snowden. From "It's Arch-itecture!", Metro, 10 March, 2004.

Wembley Stadium is designed by World Stadium Team (WST), a joint venture between HOK Sport Venue Event and Foster & Partners. The joint venture was formed in 1998, specifically to design the new Wembley Stadium.

25

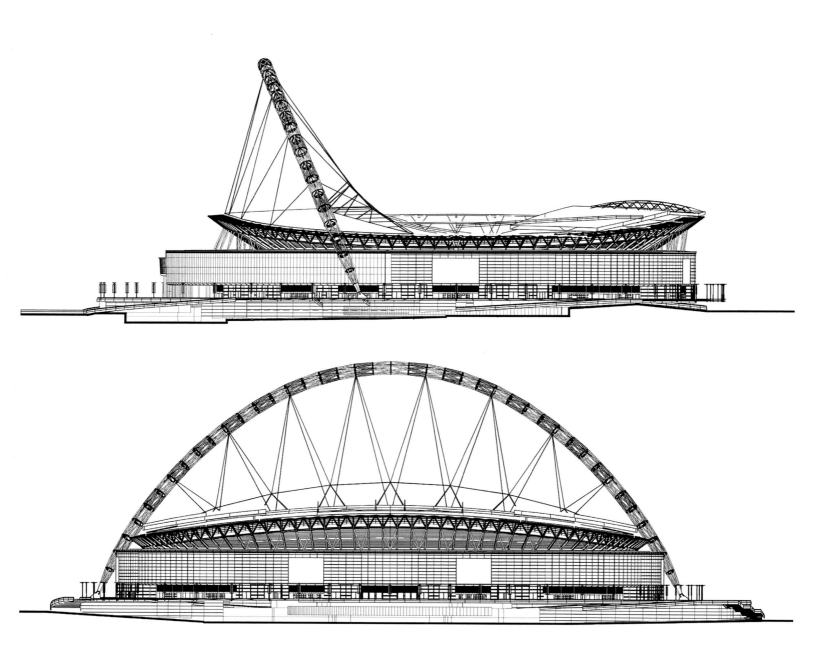

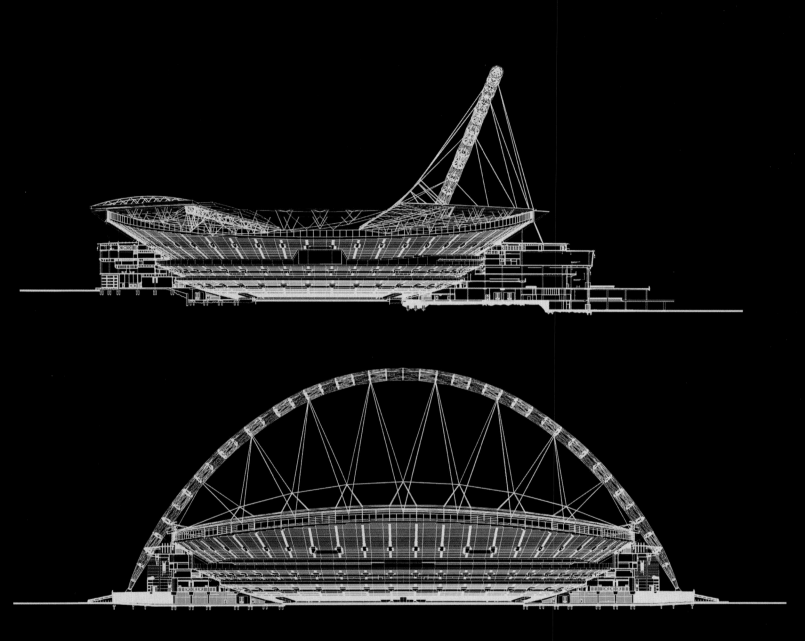

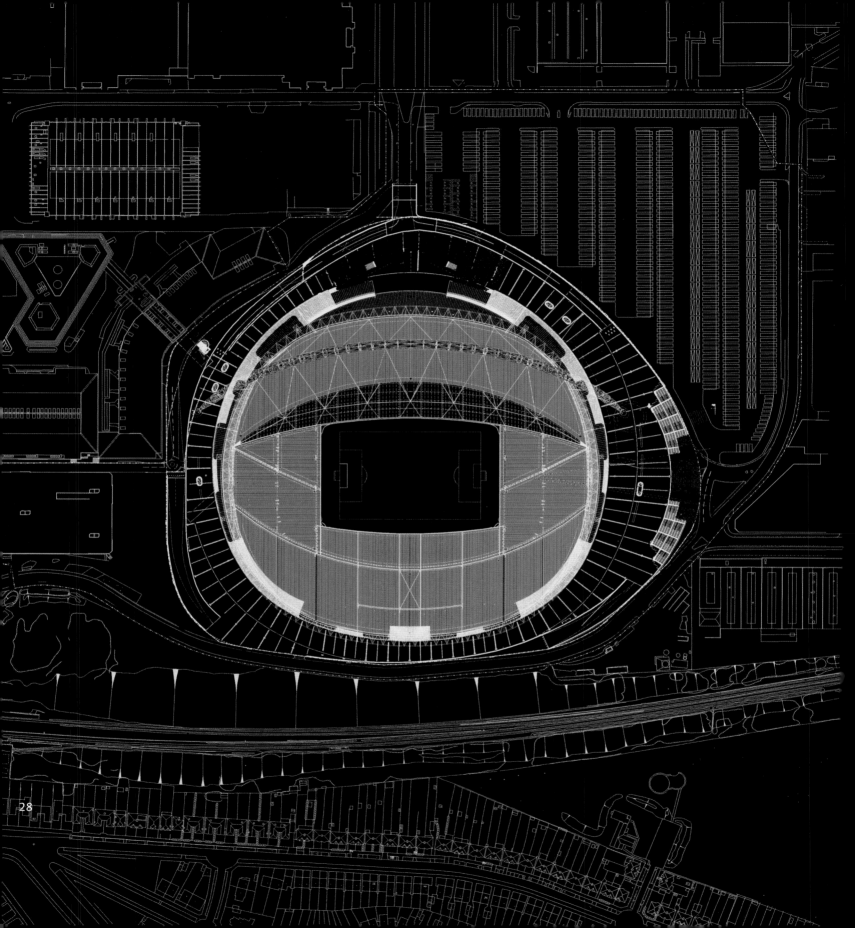

"The church of football."

Pele

"... Wembley has a special place in everyone's hearts. There is no doubt this is going to be the most spectacular stadium in the world."

Tony Blair. 2 September, 2004.

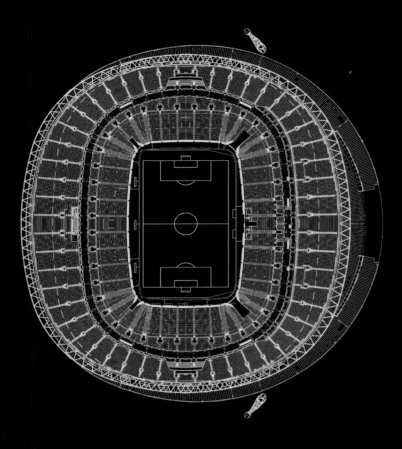

"To most players in the world, Wembley is the mecca of stadiums. To win the World Cup there would be the highlight of anyone's career."

Sir Bobby Moore

Coors Field

Denver, Colorado, USA

1995

"For its fifth year, Coors Field will look much like it did for the first four: handsome, stately and proud, its red brick façade frozen in that permanent postcard pose. Architecturally, it's still a masterpiece. Economically, it's been a great success. As a ballpark, it's one of the best in the major leagues."

The Colorado Springs Gazette. 12 April, 1999.

34

If Disneyland and Disney World were indications of America's attachment to nostalgia, there was another expression of this attitude in the emergence of New Urbanism – a movement originating in the 1980s from the Miami-based practice of Andres Duany and Elizabeth Plater-Zyberk. The movement was to take urban planning in a new direction. The firm's earliest project at Seaside, Florida, was the first authentic new town to be built successfully in the USA in over 50 years and it reflected a wave of yearning for the traditional American town, perhaps even a reaction against the very speed at which the world was changing.

   Sport was not immune to this nostalgia, and there was a distinct reaction against the functional architecture of the Houston Astrodome, Candlestick Park in San Francisco and the Busch Stadium in St. Louis. This nostalgia was evident in the choice of the ageing Los Angeles Coliseum as the venue for the 1984 Olympic Games. The multi-functional stadia of the 1960s had eradicated idiosyncrasies such as a short right field or the asymmetrical disposition of the stands, in the interest of efficiency and standardisation. But these were exactly the features that endeared the old stadia to so many baseball fans.

   The late 1980s saw a wave of nostalgia for the old type of ballpark, such as Fenway Park, home of the Boston Red Sox since 1912. One of baseball's last remaining classic ballparks, it was built to conform to the surrounding streets near Boston's Kenmore Square, with a single-level grandstand, wildly asymmetrical fences intersecting at crazy angles, and extremely close seating that placed many fans nearer home plate than any infielder. Wrigley Field, the home of the Chicago Cubs since 1916, also served as a model for the new generation of ballpark architecture, which reflects a baseball culture that is ultra-traditional, glorifies past achievements and does not welcome radical change...

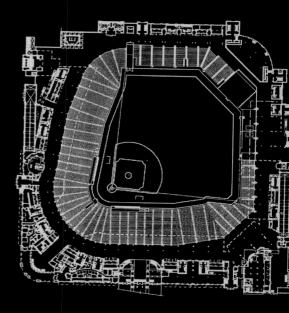

... The ballparks of the 1990s fit comfortably within the urban street scale and seek to be part of a city, rather than strike a jarring note as a dominating feature. The street façades of Coors Field integrate with the late 19th Century brick warehouse architecture of the LoDo area of downtown Denver. The graceful steelwork of the upper levels combines with the rigorous Beaux Arts massing of the podium to produce a building which exemplifies the robust environment of the American downtown.

Suncorp Stadium

Brisbane, Australia

2003

The 52,500 seat Suncorp Stadium, built on the site of the legendary Lang Park, has a continuous 'floating' steel roof, carried on four clear-span trusses supported at the corners of the stadium. The architects worked with the contours of the site, and suppressed the structure to fit the massive stadium into the context of a residential neighbourhood. Special attention has been given to the external envelope – naturally ventilated corner bays, open mesh stairwells, screens of ironbark and spotted-gum timber battens (recycled from former wharves) combine to create an overall feeling of lightness and tactile harmony. The intention was to play down the notion of the stadium as an iconic presence, though history may well make a contrary judgement.

Suncorp Stadium at Lang Park was designed by HOK Sport + Venue + Event in association with PDT Architects.

42

The intense atmosphere in the new stadium is such that it truly lives up to the long established Lang Park moniker of 'The Cauldron'. The seating hugs the field, with the closest seats 6 metres from the touchline and the rear seats just 55 metres away. The great roof amplifies the intensity at such big games as the legendary 'State of Origin' rugby league matches between Queensland and New South Wales. The open-air terraces and viewing galleries provide a modern slant on the traditional Australian verandah, giving the Suncorp Stadium a distinct regional identity, reminiscent of earlier informal areas at Australian sporting venues, with names such as the 'Outer' or the 'Hill'.

"Sports events stimulate tourism directly and indirectly by showcasing the character and attributes of the host city. In Brisbane today the dominant economic driver is not tourism, however, but long-term interstate population migration. Over a thousand people a week are persuaded to switch teams and relocate to South East Queensland, and the resulting construction and property growth powers our economy.

While we cannot attribute this mass translocation to the superior appeal of the architecture (or sport) of Queensland, we should not undervalue the very real contribution that major architectural projects make to the perceived culture and character of a city. At its best, architecture can build on and extend local patterns of urban engagement and understanding, underscore and celebrate the qualities of place, and reflect and valorize admirable local character traits and mores. From this regionalist viewpoint it is easy to understand the remarkable popular success of Suncorp Stadium."

Peter Skinner, Head of the Department of Architecture at the University of Queensland. From "Into the Cauldron", Architecture Australia, May/June, 2004.

An integral part of Suncorp Stadium's design was the incorporation of the historic Christ Church and its memorial graveyard into the stadium precinct. As rugby union is romantically referred to as 'the game they play in heaven', this rather spe-

"There is much to commend in Suncorp Stadium, from its respect for local traditions and rituals to its easy accommodation of the subtropical outdoor life. More than that, it embodies a particular set of character traits that are a source of pride and honour in Queensland sport, architecture and life. Like the legendary Lang Park heroes before it, Suncorp Stadium is neither flashy or tricky, but its unpretentious candour belies an impassioned commitment to deliver disciplined and explosive performances on the big occasions."

Peter Skinner, Head of Department of Architecture at the University of Queensland. From "Into the Cauldron", Architecture Australia, May/June, 2004.

Estádio da Luz

Lisbon, Portugal

2003

Taking cues from the local context,
the 65,000 seat Estádio da Luz,
home of the Benfica Football Club,
is defined by four bright red soaring
steel arched trusses with cable suspension: echoing Lisbon's landmark
Vasco da Gama Bridge. The arches
are supported by massive concrete
columns at the four corners of the
stadium; beneath the red arches are
four vast ovaloid roofs suspended
on steel hangers, and the leading
edges of the roofs are glazed with
transparent polycarbonate panels.
In the corners of the stadium, where
the ovaloid roof planes abut, four
transparent triangular canopies spread
like the wings of an eagle (the symbol
of Benfica FC), ensuring that every
spectator is sheltered. The two lower
decks rise steeply, with a third deck
devoted entirely to corporate spon-
sors, and the upper (fourth) deck
curves, dips and rises to its highest
points behind the goals and on the
half-way line. The Estádio da Luz
is a flamboyant celebration of light,
movement, colour and sound.

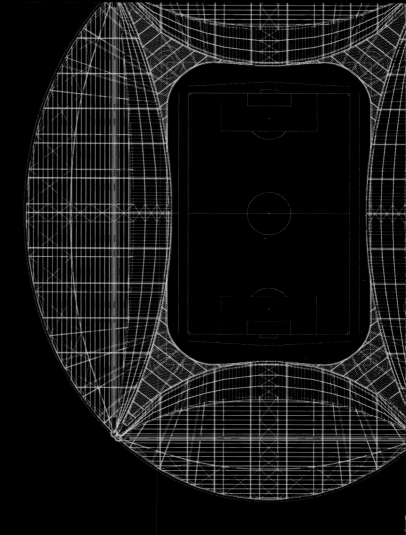

"... to football fans of a certain age the name Benfica retains the capacity to transfix. Led by Bela Guttman, the masterful Hungarian coach, the Eagles of Lisbon famously plundered Real Madrid's European crown in 1961. The next year they unleashed upon the world Eusebio, the smiling Mozambiquian hotshot. Second only to Pele, Europe's first African star blazed a trail through football's preconceptions and expectations. Although Benfica faded after defeat to Manchester United at Wembley in 1968, once sprinkled with stardust, they lived on among the greats. Even in black and white, and long before "sexy football" Benfica were luminescent.

Then there was their stadium. Wembley, Hampden, the San Siro, the Nou Camp and the Bernabeu all cast their spell at the time. But by its very title, Benfica's Estádio da Luz – Stadium of Light – suggested a playground of the gods.

A more venerable setting for a European Championship one could therefore hardly imagine."

Simon Inglis. From "Giving grounds for approval", The Times, 7 June, 2004.

53

"The mark of Benfica is hard to miss at the stadium, which has been built on some of the club's old training pitches. Benfica's striking red is the dominant colour, the roof is designed in the corners to resemble the wings of an eagle – the club's mascot – and the huge eagle statue that adorned the entrance to the old ground has been transferred to the new site.

One former Benfica president was so impressed when he saw the stadium for the first time after it opened last year that he commented: 'If God loves football, he is for sure a Benfica supporter'."

Jon Brodkin. From "Theatre of dreams and light: Luxury awaits England at Benfica's new Estádio da Luz", The Guardian, 10 June, 2004.

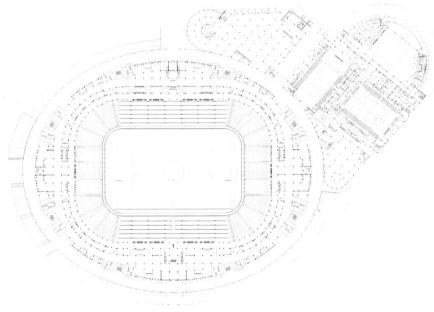

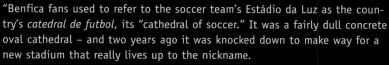

"Benfica fans used to refer to the soccer team's Estádio da Luz as the country's *catedral de futbol*, its "cathedral of soccer." It was a fairly dull concrete oval cathedral – and two years ago it was knocked down to make way for a new stadium that really lives up to the nickname.

The Benfica stadium, with its curving rings of seats and four arches rising high above, is designed to evoke the baroque style of Portugal's cathedrals."

Erik T. Burns. From "Architects Hone Their Stadium Game", Wall Street Journal Europe, 11 June, 2004.

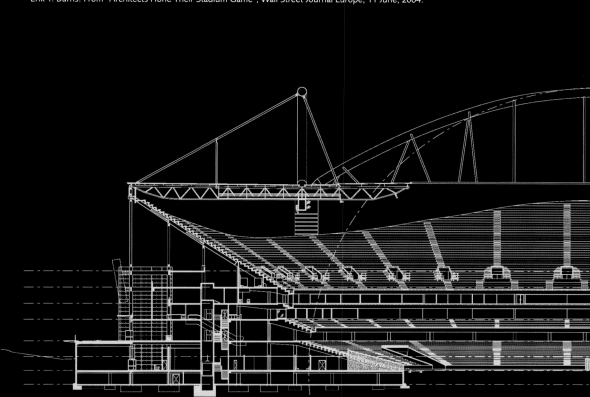

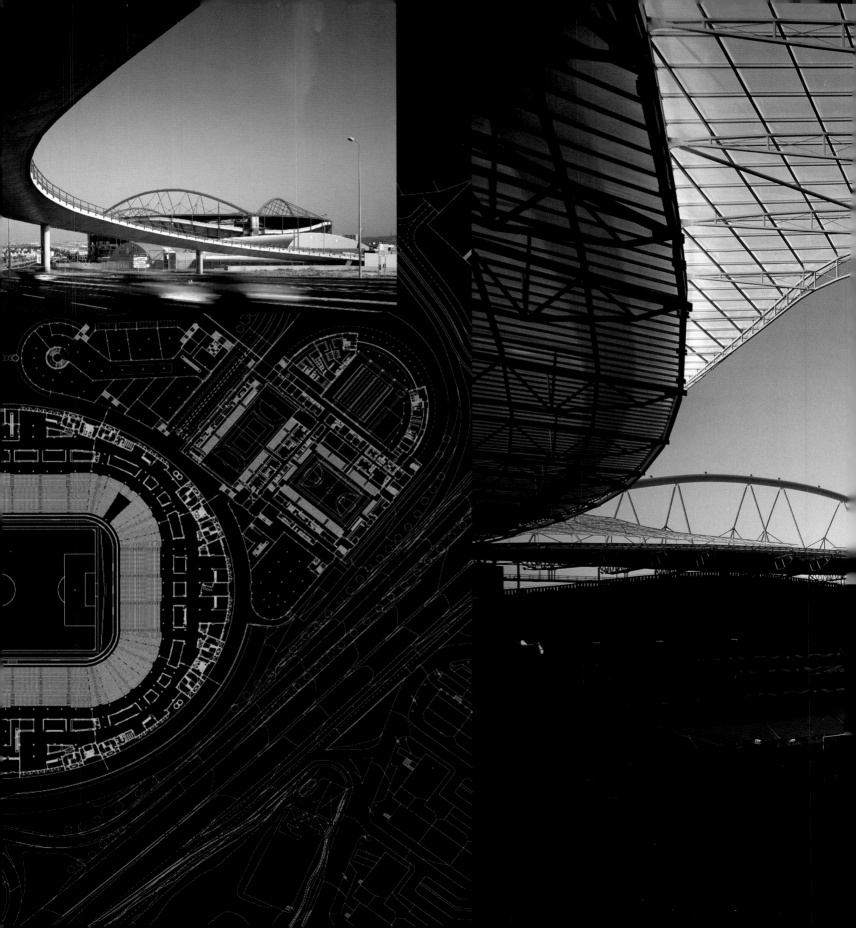

The Power of Sport

"In our daily lives, our material needs are being satisfied. Everything we buy is of a higher quality and increasingly reliable. We are being given a wider choice, but as a consequence everything is becoming very similar. The price we are paying for the satisfaction of our material needs is 'sameness'. The result has been that in the developed world people are searching, they are looking for something real in their lives, something true or something unique. The trouble is that we are all looking for it – we want a unique commodity in huge quantities!

Sport is one of the few things we have created in our society that is not predictable, it is never the same. It can be unique."

TO UNDERSTAND why stadia have become central to the lives of so many people, it is necessary to examine the role of sport in society. Sport today has moved to centrestage, effectively ousting every other form of mass entertainment. Donald Katz argues that "Sport has arguably surpassed popular music as the captivating medium most essential to being perceived as young and alive…"[1]. Sport goes straight to the hearts of people – be they spectators in the stadium or television viewers – arousing passionate and partisan behaviour. Sport has been described as "war without killing", and the language of martial conflict is employed – there are 'offence squads' and 'defence squads' in American football, we 'shoot' at goal, we celebrate 'victory' and the 'defeat' of vanquished opponents.

In the stadium, the 'field' is the focus of attention, the equivalent of the gladiatorial arena, a space of intense public scrutiny. The tension is palpable and the noise level is amplified in the enclosed space, especially when games are played under flood-lights and extraneous distractions are obliterated. The spectators are caught up in the excitement, suspense, aggression and drama on the field, and the television viewers around the globe follow every instinctive move, every well-timed strike, every weighted kick, every fingertip catch and every bone-crunching tackle. Each strategic ploy can be analysed and every error of judgement replayed. There is huge pressure to perform well and, above all, to win. The participants are the 'gods' of the modern era, the equivalent of the mythical figures of history. To quote Sarfreez Manzoor, "Sport is not an intellectual pursuit, it demands the engagement of the heart, not the brain. It is the way that men, mostly, demonstrate tribal allegiances… it is not so much a pastime as a religion complete with its cathedrals and rituals."[2] When fans identify closely with teams they experience "anxiety, frustration, anger, hostility, sadness and depression when their team does poorly and elation, ecstasy, self-fulfilment, enjoyment, self-esteem and social prestige when their team does well".[3]

1 Donald Katz (1994), quoted in Ellis Cashmore, Sports Culture: An A-Z Guide, Routledge, London, 2000. p 295.
2 Sarfrez Manzoor, "The fall of the last good man," The Guardian, UK, 14th April 2004.
3 Mary E. Duquin, "Sports and Emotions", in Handbook of Sports Studies, Edited by Jay Coakley and Eric Dunning, SAGE, London, 2002. p483.

Opposite: The Mens' 100 Metre Final in the 2000 Olympic Games. Stadium Australia (now Telstra Stadium) – Sydney, Australia.

The power of sport extends beyond the sporting field. At the 1968 Olympic Games in Mexico City, two African-American athletes, Tommie Smith and John Carlos, raised their black-gloved fists from the victor's rostrum in a protest against racial discrimination in the USA, and through their action, the athletes became symbols of a generation. Sport is so closely tied to national identity that it is inevitably linked to nation building. After the 1995 Rugby World Cup Final at Ellis Park, Johannesburg (the former citadel of Afrikaanerdom), the South African captain Francois Pienaar received the winners' trophy from President Nelson Mandela, who was wearing a replica of Pienaar's rugby shirt. The event was seen worldwide on television, and after the years of ethnic conflict provoked by the South African policy of apartheid the moment could be seen as a symbol of reconciliation. In a post match interview, Pienaar was asked, "What does it feel like to have 60,000 people behind you?" Pienaar replied, "We didn't have 60,000 people behind us, we had a nation of 43 million."[4]

The development of satellite television and the internet in the 1990s has changed our perception of sport. All the major codes thrive on international competition, and television has changed the status of a national team. As Allison Lincoln notes in Sport and Nationalism, "In the pre-television era, we had to be there to watch our national team, but television allows us all to support our national team".[5] Satellite television has created a new breed of superstars and ensured that international forms of games dominate both money and status. Teams, stadia and sports stars now have their own web sites, and the internet allows immediate access to results, previews, analyses and lives.

4 Mathew Pinsent, "Heroes Heroes", Sunday Times, London, March 28th 2004.
5 Lincoln Allison, "Sport and Nationalism", in Handbook of Sports Studies. ibid. pp346-347.

Above: Minute Maid Park (formerly Enron Field) – Houston, Texas, USA 2000

"Psychologists may be correct in their assertion that we are going through a shift from people who are 'substance driven' to people driven by a need for self-actualisation. Today we are becoming more 'inner directed'. We are seeking self-fulfilment and meaning, and we are no longer satisfied with our basic needs being 'outer directed', looking for esteem and status. This is a collective, not an individual search. We want to belong to something bigger. The values being sought are authentic not fake, rare not common or plentiful, distinctive not identical, and original not copied. To make our assessment of whether something fits within our search, we want to know the story behind it. We want to know why we should buy the product. This desire for the story is where sport comes into the picture. Sport is the ultimate story, constantly changing, never predictable. Sports stories appear every day in the newspapers and on TV, not just documenting the results from the previous day, but revelling in the drama of a drugs test, an extramarital affair, or the comeback of a player from a crippling injury. When that player gets back on the pitch, we know their story and we are then involved. Sport supplies the stories that make life worth living for many people."

The globalisation of sport, resulting from the advent of satellite television, is paralleled by the creation of multinational teams. For example, Arsenal FC in the English Premier League currently has a French manager, Arsene Wenger, and a squad of approximately 40 players drawn from 16 countries representing Europe, Africa, Asia and South America. This phenomenon is invaluable when 'branding' a football team for international markets. In May 2004, the Thai Prime Minister Thaksin Shinawatra sought to acquire a 30% stake in Liverpool FC.[6] "Lots of our products need a brand," said Thaksin, "and Liverpool is one that we can use on the world market. It is an established club that is popular in Asia."

Sport has developed to become the world's major global culture, extending its reach to embrace all people, regardless of religion, race or colour, and sport can be seen as a model for international relations. The dream of world peace is, to quote Kendall Blanchard, "well served by efforts to understand sporting diversity, encourage international cooperation and revisit the spirit of the Olympics".[7] In an increasingly secular world where the major religious symbols have become divisive or have lost their impact, sport has become a signifier of shared values and aspirations.

6 John Aglionby, "Kop Thai", The Guardian, 11th May 2004.
7 Kendall Blanchard, The Anthropology of Sport, in Handbook of Sports Studies, ibid.

Above: SBC Park (formerly Pacific Bell Park) – San Francisco, California, USA 2000

"Perhaps this is an old hippie idea of the world community, but the concept of caring about what someone on the other side of the world is thinking, or a concern for what they are going through, is now more real than ever before. The common language is sport. It means as much to an Englishman to win the Rugby World Cup as it does to an Australian. And it means as much to a Brazilian to win the Soccer World Cup as it does to a German. They have something in common; they have a shared value system, giving structure to the world community."

The Codification of Sport

The 19th Century development of organised games in Britain paralleled the Industrial Revolution, which so indelibly changed the social landscape. A clear connection can be observed between rapid urbanisation, the growth of population and the codification of sport. The vast movement of people from the countryside to the cities created a critical mass for the development of organised sport. This pattern would later be repeated in Western Europe, North America, South America, Australia and Asia.

Both association football (soccer) and rugby football stem from common roots, and these two games subsequently influenced the American form of football and the Australian Rules version.[8] Various violent and disorganized forms of football flourished in the British Isles from as early as the 8th Century, but the sea-change occurred at the beginning of the 19th Century, when football (with a basic set of rules) was adopted by a number of English public schools.

The contemporary history of soccer dates back to the 26th October 1863, when representatives of 11 London clubs and schools met, intent on establishing a standard set of regulations to govern the matches played amongst them. As a result of this meeting, the two codes of rugby football and association football (soccer) went their separate ways. It marked the emergence of the Football Association (FA) and following further codification, the game of soccer expanded at a phenomenal rate.[9]

After its split from association football, rugby was codified as the Rugby Football Union in 1871. The game soon spread to France, Scotland, Wales, Ireland, Australia, New Zealand and South Africa, and to countries such as Argentina where there were large expatriate communities. By 1886 the International Rugby Football Union (RFU) was established, but the RFU was barely 30 years old when 22 clubs in the north of England split from the parent body on the issue of payment to players for 'broken time'.[10] A meeting took place at the George Hotel in Huddersfield on August 29th 1895, and the clubs in favour of paying their players went their separate way, forming the Northern Union (Rugby Football League). The separation was along social and class lines, and rugby league (as it became known) still retains the aura of the 'working man's' game while rugby union finds it difficult to shed its middle class image. This perception has changed slightly since 1995, when rugby union also became a professional sport.

As early as the 1850s, rugby football was played (by a largely British migrant population) in Australia and New Zealand, and it also established itself in South Africa. It can be observed that the game was particularly suited to the sports ethic of these robust young nations. Following the split with rugby union in England, rugby league established itself in Sydney in 1908, with the first grand final played between South Sydney and Balmain.

A new version of football was born in 1857, when Tom Wills, a member of the Melbourne Cricket Club, returned to Australia after schooling in England where he was football captain of Rugby School. He advocated the winter game of football as a

8 The Chinese are credited with the earliest form of football in approximately 255 - 206 BC. The game was called Tsu'Chu and there are records of this game in military manuals dating back to the Tsin Dynasty (255 - 206 BCE). Another form of the game was the Japanese Kemari. It was played for the first time in the 7th Century. Sepak Takraw is played in Malaysia, Indonesia and other Southeast Asian countries with a net like volleyball. The ball is made of rattan or cane and can only be played with the feet and head. It evolved from the earlier game of Sepak Raga.
9 In the 15 years between 1874 and 1889, 50 of the 92 clubs (54%) that presently constitute the four senior divisions of the English Football (Soccer) League were founded. The peak period was 1883 to 1887 when no fewer than 23 of today's top English soccer teams were founded. www.footballnetwork.org
10 Rugby league in England has always been associated with northern industrial cities. Famous teams such as Wigan, St. Helens, Halifax, Bradford, Leeds, Huddersfield, Hull, Whitehaven and Workington grew out of close-knit communities in Lancashire, Yorkshire, Cumberland and Westmoreland. Rugby League players insisted they should be paid for missing a Saturday afternoon work shift and this was unacceptable within the amateur Rugby Union code.

Above: Stadium Australia (now Telstra Stadium) – Sydney, Australia 1999.

these teams dominated the game for most of the first 100 years of football in the USA. Today, despite greatly increased interest in professional football, more than 35 million spectators attend intercollegiate contests – played by some 640 teams each year. Many college stadiums hold more than 50,000 spectators, and one stadium, at the University of Michigan, holds more than 100,000.

The professional game attracted only limited public support during its first 30 years, but in 1920 the American Professional Football Association (APFA) was formed (renamed the National Football League (NFL) in 1922). Professional football then attracted larger numbers of first-rate college players, and this increased patronage made the league economically viable. In 1933, the NFL split into two divisions, and later that year, the Chicago Bears, champions of the Western Division, defeated the New York Giants, champions of the Eastern Division, for the first professional football title. The American Football League (AFL) was formed in 1960, and the champions of the AFL and the NFL first met in the AFL–NFL World Championship Game of 1967. The AFL merged with the NFL in 1970, and the end of season play-off was renamed the Super Bowl. It remains the most important single-day sporting event in the United States.

Cricket has existed in Britain since the reign of King Edward I in the 13th Century. The first major official match was Kent v Middlesex in 1719, and the earliest known Laws of Cricket (the 'Code of 1744') give the length of the pitch as 22 yards (or 20.1168 metres), which is one chain or one tenth of a furlong. It actually approximates to the width of a Saxon field or 'strip'. The Marylebone Cricket Club (MCC) was formed in May 1787, and a year later, the Club laid down a Code of Laws, detailing how players could be given out. These laws were adopted throughout the game – and the MCC remains the authority and arbiter of laws relating to cricket around the world.

Cricket was transported to Australia, South Africa, New Zealand and the West Indies, but it did not put down roots in the USA. Americans preferred the game of baseball – a sport descended from the traditional English pastime of rounders. In 1845 Alexander Cartwright (and members of a New York club known as the Knickerbocker Club) devised the first rules and regulations for the modern game. Cartwright set the bases 90 feet

way of keeping cricketers fit during the off-season. Along with three other MCC members he devised an entirely new game based on the Rugby School rules, which were modified to be played on an oval pitch. The rules of this new game were established in May 1859, and came to be known as Australian (Aussie) Rules football.[11]

A new game also emerged in the USA. The birth date of American football is generally recognised as November 6, 1869, when teams from Rutgers and Princeton Universities met in New Brunswick, New Jersey, for the first intercollegiate football game. In the early games, each team used 25 players at a time, though by 1873 the number was reduced to 20 players, and in 1876 to 15 players. The game resembled rugby football as played in English public schools, but in 1879, Walter Camp, a player and coach at Yale University, wrote the American Football rules, which broke completely with the English game. He also reduced the number of players on each side to 11. The scoring system was clarified over the next four years, and by 1883, touchdowns were counted in addition to goals. American football was initially made popular by teams representing colleges and universities, and

11 The game this group codified became known as Melbourne Rules Football. The rules that most differentiated it from rugby were rule six, which allowed and defined a mark and the resultant free kick, and rule eight, which said the ball could be carried when marked or caught from a bounce. It could not be lifted from the ground. The game is played with an oval ball. A few years later, a rule forcing players to bounce the ball every 10 metres was introduced.
12 In 1888 the Lawn Tennis Association (UK) was formed and in 1906 the Wimbledon Championships began.

13 In 1891 Basketball was invented in Massachusetts and the following year the first formal rules were established. Boxing was provided with rules formulated by the Marquis of Queensbury in England in 1857. Hockey is said to have been played in some form since 2000 BC but it would be only in 1861 that the first hockey club was founded at Blackheath in London. Another version of hockey - Ice Hockey – was played at Victoria skating rink in Montreal in March 1875 and in 1904 the International Pro Hockey League was set up. Gaelic Football has its own colourful history and in 1884 the Gaelic Athletic Association was formed. In 1885 the GAA rules were drawn up and just two years

apart in a diamond configuration. He decided that there should be nine players on each team and decreed the positions on the field. Each team would get three 'outs' and then switch sides. A 90-degree angle would be used to determine if a ball was playable. The first organised game took place on June 1845 at Elysian Field in New Jersey between the Knickerbocker Club and the New York Nine.

The late 19th Century and early 20th Century saw the codification of every other major sport. Tennis originated in 1592 with the French game of *paume*, but the modern game was devised in 1868 when the All England Lawn Tennis & Croquet Club was established, and in 1877 the first recorded tennis championships were held at Wimbledon.[12] The International Lawn Tennis Federation was set up in October 1912, and in January 1924 the Rules of Tennis were adopted. Basketball, Ice Hockey, and Boxing also became popular in the expanding cities, and all were codified between 1857 and 1891.[13]

Horse racing became a professional sport in England during the reign of Queen Anne (1702-14)[14]. In 1750 the racing elite met at Newmarket to form the Jockey Club, which exercises control over English racing. The Jockey Club wrote the rules of racing and sanctioned racecourses to conduct meetings under those rules. British settlers took horses and horse racing with them to America, and in 1894 the nation's most prominent track and stable owners met in New York to form the American Jockey Club, in order to regulate horse racing in the USA

---

later, in 1887, the All-Ireland championships were held.
14 The competitive racing of horses had its origins among the prehistoric nomadic tribesmen of Central Asia who first domesticated the horse about 4500 BC. The origins of modern racing lie in the 12th Century, when English knights returned from the Crusades with swift Arab horses. Over the next 400 years, an increasing number of Arab stallions were imported and bred to English and Irish mares to produce horses that combined speed and endurance.

Above and opposite: Jacobs Field – Cleveland, Ohio, USA 1994

Ascot Racecourse

Ascot, England

2006 (scheduled completion)

A completely new 30,000 seat grandstand at Ascot Racecourse will incorporate 272 private boxes, including the Royal box. Plans were completed in 2003 and construction started in summer 2004, after demolition of the existing grandstand

The grandstand sits on the brow of a hill with panoramic views of the course to the north and of Windsor Great Park beyond. The form of the building is a 480 metre shallow-arched hyperbolic paraboloid with a fabric roof. It is stepped to take the form of a gentle mound, and conceptually it is 'a building between trees', with a slight curve on plan to embrace the racecourse.

A racecourse grandstand is essentially a daytime building, but up-lighting at Ascot will create a magical experience at twilight. The aim is to create a building that will be the embodiment of the 'Royal Ascot' brand, and a colourful theatrical experience in its own right.

The grounds of Ascot Racecourse have numerous superb trees, and the soaring steel structure of the cathedral-like galleria was inspired by the forms of these trees. The large atrium acts as an 'environmental lung' for the grandstand, which will be topped by a lightweight glass and steel roof.

"Ascot – one of the most prestigious racecourses in the world – is to undergo a £180 million transformation with a new grandstand, a royal enclosure and parade ring, the Evening Standard can reveal today.

The famous straight mile of turf, on which the Queen parades during Royal Ascot each year, will be moved to allow the futuristic grandstand to be built.

Lord Hartington, Her Majesty's representative at Ascot and Chairman of the Ascot Authority, said: 'I am delighted to have unveiled today what we believe is an outstanding new facility, ensuring Ascot's place as the finest racecourse in the world. Our plans take advantage of the best that modern architecture, structural engineering and building technology can offer, while preserving the unique appeal of Ascot.'

Ascot's chief executive, Douglas Erskine-Crum, said: 'We want to demystify racing and bring the racegoers close to their heroes. The Queen has been kept regularly informed of the plans and appears to be content with the progress made so far'."

Patrick Sawer. From "Ascot's £180m new look", Evening Standard, 27 June, 2002.

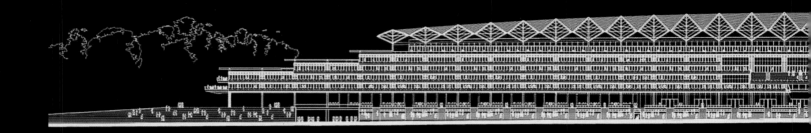

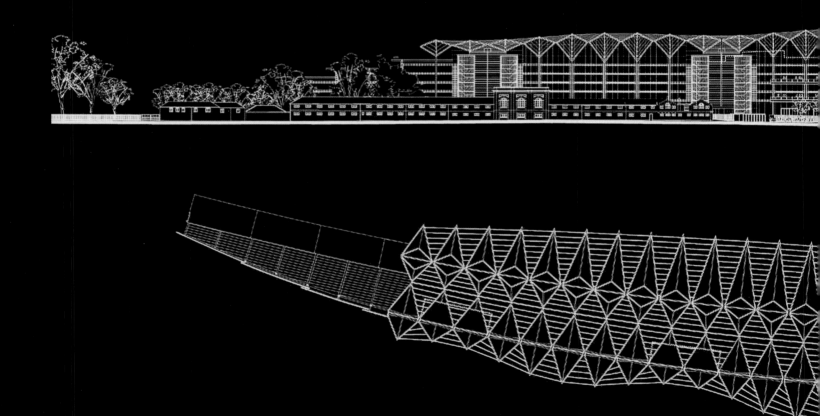

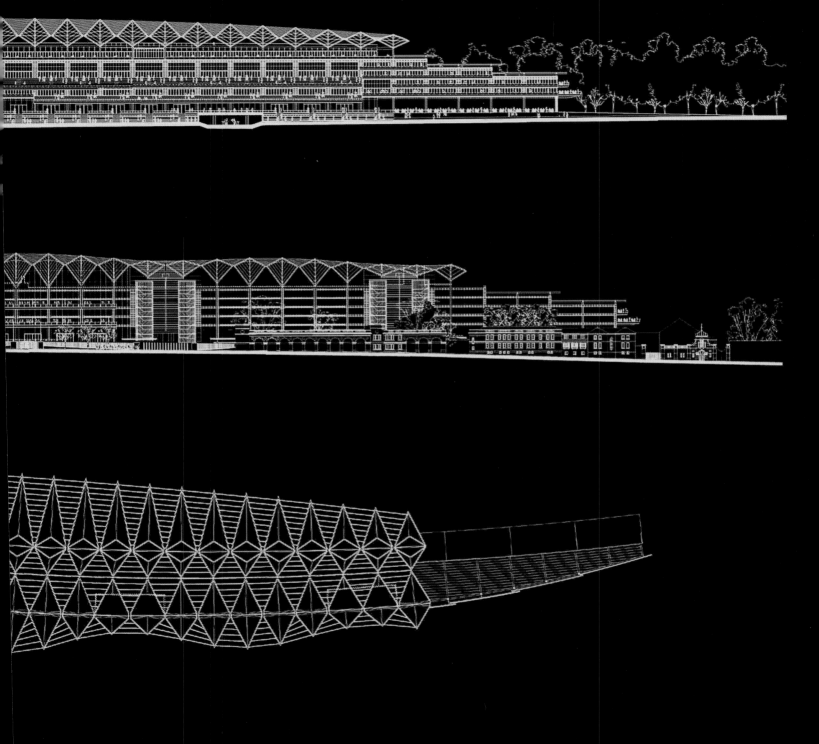

All England Lawn Tennis and Croquet Club

Wimbledon, London, England

2006 (scheduled completion)

As with horse racing, tennis has been relatively slow to adjust to the demands of digital television, but in January 2004 the All England Lawn Tennis and Croquet Club gave the go-ahead for a roof over Wimbledon's centre court. The capacity will be expanded from 13,800 to 15,000. Wimbledon was facing pressure from other international tennis venues, which had already installed roofs to ensure that play continues during bad weather, although the Australian Open is currently the only Grand Slam event played beneath a retractable roof. Much of the pressure for change has come from satellite television, which pays handsomely for the live coverage of international tennis.

The new hydraulically operated roof – a "folding fabric concertina" – will measure 65 metres x 70 metres. The structure works on a principle similar to an umbrella, with metal ribs supporting a translucent fabric designed to last 20 years and floodlights will be installed on the 10 steel trusses supporting this fabric. The roof will open or close in under 10 minutes, and can be folded into a very compressed area when not in use.

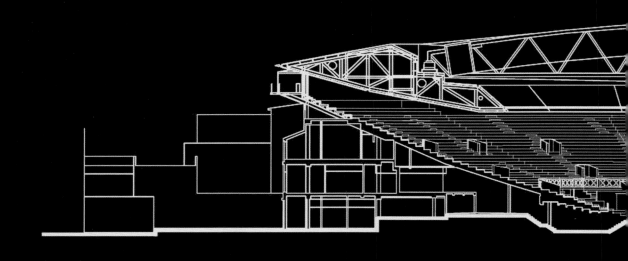

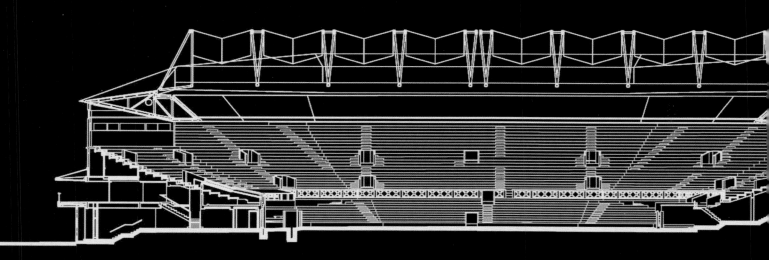

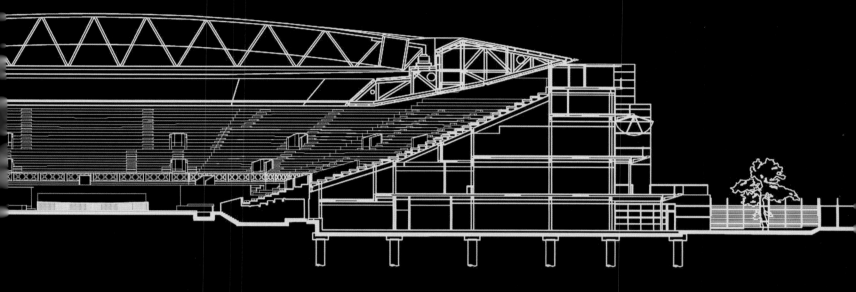

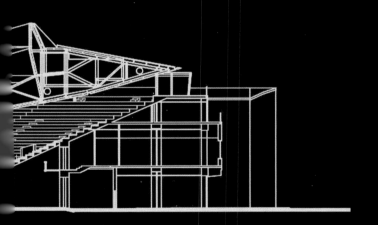

"Centre Court has been our jewel in the crown for over 80 years. Our innovative plans seek to retain the history and tradition of Centre Court, but with outstanding new facilities for the players, spectators and television audiences of the 21st Century."

Tim Phillips, Chairman of the All England Lawn Tennis and Croquet Club.

Reliant Stadium

Houston, Texas, USA

2002

The 72,000 seat Reliant Stadium is the most expensive stadium (per seat) ever built in the USA, and it dwarfs the adjacent Astrodome – the landmark stadium of the 1960s. The new stadium, home of the Houston Texans and the Houston Rodeo, hosted the 2004 Super Bowl (memorable for Janet Jackson's 'wardrobe malfunction'), and is the first NFL venue to have a retractable roof with a natural grass playing surface.

The transparent fabric roof consists of two large panels: each panel slides on a track and rests over the end zone on two massive 'super trusses', which span the length of the field. The trusses, tapering between 15 metres (50ft) deep at mid-span and 21 metres (72ft) at the end supports, are supported by four giant reinforced columns or 'super columns' – one at each corner of the field. The trusses, spanning approximately 206 metres (675ft) between supports, have a trapezoid-shaped cross section. They cantilever over the top of the supporting columns for approximately 38 metres (125ft) at each end, providing support for the rolling roof panels in their retracted position.

81

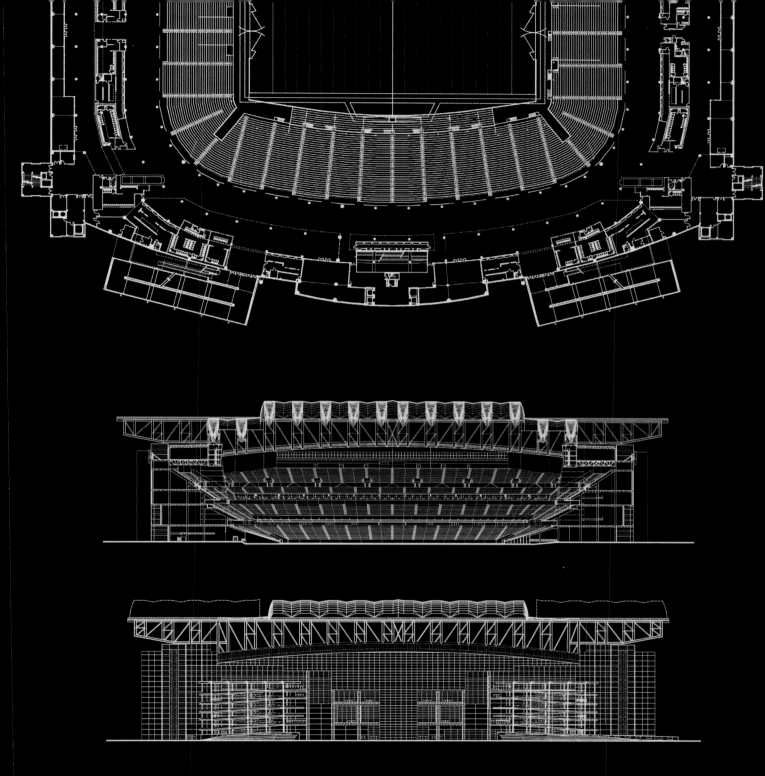

Houston is an heroic city with great aspirations: its people, its ideas and its buildings are larger than life. The colossal scale of the trusses and the cantilevered roof structure of Reliant Stadium are suitably suggestive of a gigantic ocean oil-drilling platform or rocket launching facility.

83

Oriole Park at Camden Yards

Baltimore, Maryland, USA

1992

"Oriole Park at Camden Yards incorporates all the modern conveniences – for fans and ballplayers – without sacrificing history, tradition or aesthetics. It brings the game closer to the fans, giving the crowd a more intimate look at the game. It restored uniqueness and single-purpose as attainable and desirable goals. It has become the most influential major-league ballpark since Yankee Stadium."

The Detroit News, April 12, 1999.

"Nowhere on Earth does the [Seattle] Kingdome seem more inadequate a place to watch baseball, more soulless and just plain wrong, than from right here in the green plastic seats behind home plate at Oriole Park at Camden Yards. It has nothing to do with the nifty cup-holder at every seat, or the food options or the state-of-the-art JumboTRON beyond center field.

Rather, follow the trajectory of the ball as it comes off the bat of Bret Barberie with two out, bases loaded and the Orioles' game with the Texas Rangers tied in the bottom of the ninth. It floats up, past the redbrick B&O Warehouse, into the infinite Baltimore evening sky, white leather on black canvas. Then, on its way down, it draws a path that uses the city as a backdrop, like the set of a play that runs 81 times a year (and sometimes longer).

The ball passes in front of the modern skyscrapers several blocks in the distance, then the antique Bromo-Seltzer tower with its Big Ben-like clock, finally setting down in a cushion of bluegrass in short center field, mere feet from where Babe Ruth's father ran a saloon early in the century.

Baltimore wins! Baltimore – not just the Oriole ballclub – wins!"

Tom Farrey. From The Seattle Times, 20 August, 1995.

The design of Oriole Park took its cues from the historic B&O Railway Station and a warehouse running along the eastern boundary of the site, parallel with the former rail tracks. The stadium has a three-storey brick podium with a lighter steel structure set above. The colours are pale buff bricks (like the old railway buildings) and dark green ironwork, not unlike the colour and structure of the cranes operating along Baltimore's water-front. The field is set seven metres below the external ground level to improve the relationship of the stadium to adjacent buildings.

Oriole Park proved to be extraordi-narily popular with baseball fans, and rival ballpark owners were inevitably attracted to the concept. Other base-ball stadia followed, using a similar traditional language; taking cues from the dominant materials of the area, and introducing noticeable regional variations in response to the specific site context. The idiosyncrasies of the old ballparks began to creep back into the new plans, which were a reaction to the 'cookie-cutter' stadia of the 1960s and 1970s.

Millennium Stadium

Cardiff, Wales

1999

Millennium Stadium was built for the 1999 Rugby World Cup on the site of the existing Cardiff Arms Park, the home of Welsh rugby. Although one of the most famous sporting venues in the world, Cardiff Arms had no presence in the city, it was un-noticeable. The new stadium was designed as an 'icon', and it would kick-start Cardiff's urban regeneration. It is the new home of the Welsh Rugby Union, and is now regarded as the best rugby stadium in the world. It has served as the unofficial headquarters of English soccer, while Wembley Stadium is being rebuilt, and it has also been remarkably successful as a venue for concerts and festivals.

The stadium has 72,500 seats under Britain's first fully retractable roof, which is 120 metres long and closes within 20 minutes. The architectural priority was to retain the 'cauldron' atmosphere of Cardiff Arms Park, with a close, almost intimate, connection between the players and the spectators. The stadium's vibrant red and green colour scheme is an expression of the growing national pride of Wales.

"Millennium Stadium is the best thing to have happened to Cardiff and Wales for a generation and will be an inspiration for us all, a sense of national pride and trigger for economic and environmental regeneration. It is a huge confidence boost and with the 1999 World Cup is a fitting landmark for the Millennium and will create a fabulous platform to project Wales to the world.

The stadium will be the engine of prosperity for the next 50 years, attracting new prosperity and tens of thousands of visitors to Cardiff and Wales, and helping to regenerate large areas of the heart of the Welsh capital.

From "Cardiff Leads The World" in 'At Your Service', a detail of services provided by Cardiff County Council. April, 1996.

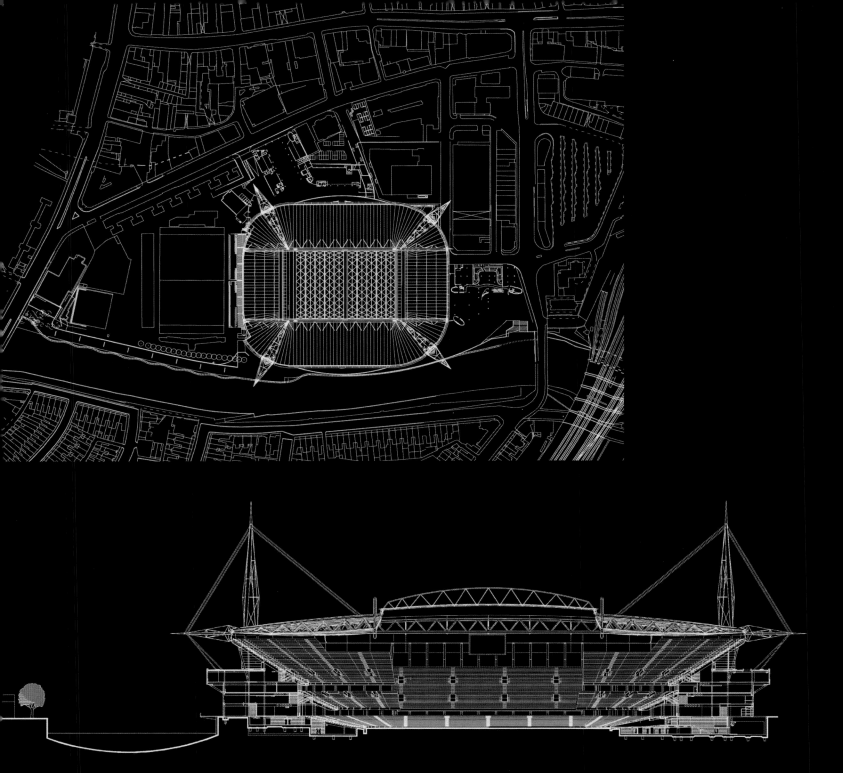

Millennium Stadium sits comfortably in its urban context, yet the dramatic white steel masts form an immediately identifiable landmark wherever you go in Cardiff. The stadium has become a focus for the regeneration of the inner city, with the shops and hotels thriving on match-day weekends.

"Stadia evoke the strongest of emotions, not just because of the events that take place in them but because of the buildings themselves.

The opening day of the Millennium Stadium in Cardiff was very emotional: the sell-out crowd approached the venue with heads craned back to take in this monumental addition to their city, and when they entered the huge bowl they paused. If ever there was a moment when 'wow' could be used to express an emotion, that was it."

Rod Sheard

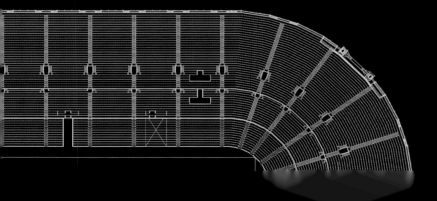

"Millennium Stadium will give Europe's youngest capital city a riverside environment to match its continental rivals through the creation of the Taff Riverside Walk. Unlocking the potential of the River Taff for leisure and tourism development was an important component of the stadium project. This new riverside development will allow direct links by boat from Cardiff Bay, reaching into the heart of the capital and providing a major attraction for visitors and local people alike."

From "Cardiff Leads The World" in 'At Your Service', a detail of services provided by the Cardiff County Council. April, 1996.

Five Generations of Stadia

"The 'Five Generations' theory evolved from practical observations of the way that the development of stadia has changed over the years. It is important that the forces which have driven the development of stadia over the last two decades are understood, along with an appreciation of how stadia can now contribute to the growth of sustainable communities."

THE THEORY of 'Five Generations' of stadia is not a simple description of the chronological development of stadia; there is substantial overlap between generations, and some stadia straddle the generational boundaries. It is still possible to find Second and Third Generation models being built in some parts of the world, where the developers are constrained by budget, by infrastructural limitations, or by the size and development of the fan base.

The precedents for modern stadia can be found in ancient Greece and Rome. The Greek form was dictated by the site, and stadia either occupied the floor of a valley with the spectators using the natural slopes for seating, or they were built on the shoulder of a hill with the upper slopes forming the seating. Essentially they were embedded in the topography, and the spectators had a panoramic vista over the landscape. This model was used at Delphi, Epidauros and Olympus.[1] The Roman form was the antithesis of this, and amphitheatres, such as the Colosseum in Rome (80AD), dominated the landscape.[2] The Roman stadium was oval in shape and was encompassed by substantial façades. The attention of the spectator was focused inwards on the intense and frequently violent action, and there was no opportunity for the contemplation of nature. Whereas the Greek stadium was essentially rural, the Roman version was an urban form.

These two models became powerful determinants of stadium morphology in the late 19th Century, when sports were codified and the designers sought precedents. The Greek model was suited to a more leisurely contemplation of sporting events which lasted for several hours or even days, and was therefore adapted for early cricket grounds and racecourses. The Roman model was eminently more suited to the 'cauldrons' of soccer, rugby and American football where the length of play is relatively short and the action is very aggressive. Early baseball parks and Australian Rules football grounds were a hybrid of both types.

1 The Olympic Games was the most important of all Greek festivals and united the disparate Greek City States with the proclamation of ekecheiria (suspension of hostilities) for a three-month period. The Olympic Games continued for 1100 years, from 776 B.C. until ended in 394 A.D. by the Emperor Theodosius who was antagonistic to the idea of athletics.
2 Stadia were central to Roman cultural life. Chariot racing dates back at least to the 6th Century BC. The largest racing track in Rome was the Circus Maximus, surrounded on three sides by stands (originally wooden but later made of stone) seating approximately 150,000 spectators.

Above: Millennium Stadium – Cardiff, Wales 1999

First Generation Stadia

"The history of the modern stadium dates back to the codification of sport in the second half of the 19th Century. The First Generation of stadia placed the emphasis on accommodating large numbers of spectators, with minimal concern for the quality of the facilities or the comfort of those spectators."

From the last days of the Roman Empire until the Victorian era in Britain, the stadium as a building category lapsed into oblivion and no significant stadia were built for approximately 1,500 years. There were sporting activities in pre-industrial Europe, such as jousting, fencing, archery, horse racing, wrestling and bare-knuckle fighting, but none of the tournaments were large enough to justify the building of permanent stadia. At most, they would have a temporary stand for the nobility and clergy. All this changed with the coming of the Industrial Revolution. The construction of sporting venues, which can be collectively referred to as First Generation stadia, was instigated by the huge crowds of spectators attracted to the newly codified sports of soccer, rugby football, cricket, American football and Australian Rules football.

The early venues were essentially large 'bowls' and there were few amenities. Toilets were rudimentary, and only the club's directors and a relatively small number of spectators were seated in grandstands fashioned from brick, iron and timber, with corrugated iron sheets providing overhead protection from the elements. The vast majority of the spectators stood on open terraces, sometimes constructed in concrete, at other times fashioned from recycled railway sleepers or compacted colliery slag. It could be extraordinarily bleak in mid-January in Europe and the USA, and it required a great deal of fortitude to support one's local team.

This basic form of stadia was the norm in Britain until the 1960s but, in spite of the basic facilities, the crowds attracted to soccer were huge.[3] In much of the UK, soccer was virtually the only form of entertainment, and fierce rivalry developed between clubs in the same city or region. The scale of the early football grounds was impressive, but the majority lacked any distinct architectural qualities as they were developed incrementally, with stands being added in a piecemeal manner. The basic aim was to accommodate as many fans as possible, and little architectural care was lavished on the external façades as the grounds were mainly private facilities, usually surrounded by terrace houses, railway sidings and industrial sites.

This initial burst of stadium building in Britain was matched by developments in Europe. A number of European stadia, particularly in Italy and Germany, were planned as part of a municipally owned sports complex and these were far removed from the typical British First Generation model. One shining example of the potential for stadium design was the Stadio Communale in Florence (1930-1932) designed by Pier Luigi Nervi. The design embraced Modernist architectural principles, and while the stadium itself was a simple concrete bowl, it featured an elegant grandstand with cantilevered curved concrete roof beams, signalling "a great leap forward in stadium design".[4] Other grandstands constructed in the 1930s in a Modernist architectural language included the barrel-vaulted

Opposite: Crowd at Villa Park in Birmingham, England, watching Aston Villa v Birmingham City, October 1930.

3. The record attendance at Highbury was 73,295, at Molyneux 76,588, at Old Trafford 76,962, at Goodison Park 78,299, at Chelsea's Stamford Bridge 82,905, and at Maine Road Manchester 84,569 (the Football League record attendance). In Scotland 149,415 spectators watched Scotland play England at Hampden Park in 1937 – a record for an international in Europe.
4 Simon Inglis, The Football Grounds of Europe, Willow Books, London, 1990.

Stade de Lescure at Bordeaux (1938) and Feyenoord's functional steel-framed DeKuip Stadium in Rotterdam (1937). Possibly the most architecturally distinguished sporting structure was the grandstand designed by Eduardo Torroja in 1935 for the Zarzuela racetrack in Madrid.

The design of cricket grounds generally followed the Greek model, responsive to the topography and the landscape.[5] The first in England was the Marylebone Cricket Club (MCC) ground in St John's Wood, London (1814), known as Lords, after its founder Thomas Lord. The ground attracted large numbers of spectators who sat on the ground around the boundary. In 1889, William Nicholson, a gin distiller, sponsored the construction of the handsome brick Pavilion, replacing a small pavilion on the same site. The Victorian structure is now a listed building and one of the landmarks of world sport. The Oval, the headquarters of the Surrey County Cricket Club (SCCC) was set up on land leased from the Duchy of Cornwall in 1845. A dignified Members' Pavilion (1898) was built in brick and masonry topped by a clock and twin cupolas.[6] The architect for the pavilion was A T Muirhead, who was also responsible for the design of a pavilion for the Lancashire County Cricket Club at Old Trafford, Manchester. Erected in 1894, it was a beautiful three-tiered brick Victorian pavilion with two copper-clad cupolas. Inevitably, these grounds, located on the fringes of cities, were engulfed by urban expansion. A gasholder and blocks of flats now overshadow the Oval in South London. As the game spread around the globe, cricket grounds were built in Sri Lanka, India, South Africa, the West Indies and Zimbabwe. These grounds were very simple venues where the majority of spectators sat on open terraces or earth mounds. When grandstands were built, they were often imposing iron and wood structures on a brick or concrete base.

Australian First Generation stadia were usually multi-purpose venues surrounded by banked earth berms, upon which spectators sat or stood. Traditionally, these grass-covered embankments were named 'The Hill' or 'The Outer'. The Sydney Cricket Ground (SCG) at Moore Park dates back to 1810 and has been used for cricket, rugby league and Australian Rules. The ground has two surviving 19th Century grandstands – the beautiful Members Pavilion built in 1886 and the Ladies Stand, erected in 1896. The Melbourne Cricket Ground (MCG) was established in 1853 and has become the principal venue and spiritual home for Australian Rules football (now known as the AFL) as well as Australian cricket.[7] A huge concrete bowl for much of its life, the MCG has seen many changes and is currently being redeveloped in time for the 2006 Commonwealth Games. In New Zealand, First Generation stadia were generally multi-use venues, with the national obsession with rugby union being the major consideration. In 1874, just three years after rugby union was codified in Britain, Carisbrook Park was built in Dunedin, and the notorious Athletic Park in Wellington hosted its first Rugby Union test match in 1903. An incredibly bleak and intimidating stadium with an icy wind blowing up from Antarctica, the New Zealand All Blacks habitually capitalised on the bone-chilling conditions to crush test match opponents.

Following its codification, baseball became the game of choice for Americans. The venues were initially quite small and spartan; the Polo Grounds in New York (1891) accommodated just 16,000 spectators. But attendance at major league games climbed from 4.7 million in 1903 to 10 million in 1911, and as a consequence there was a colossal boom in ballpark construction from 1909 to 1916. Among the new ballparks were Comiskey Park in Chicago (1910), and Ebbets Field in Boston (1913). More attention was given to the external façade of the ballpark than with early European sporting grounds. Comiskey Park "adopted a virile warehouse vocabulary… enlivened with geometric decoration" while Ebbets Field "was wrapped in a Renaissance brick shell with pilasters, detached columns and Corinthian half-capitals…"[8] These early ballparks demonstrate memorable architecture as a result of the dialogue between the spatial requirements of the game and the urban texture of the ballpark's neighborhood, and each ballpark had its own idiosyncrasies as a result of this dialogue. After World War I, baseball increased in popularity and huge new stadia were required. The Yankee Stadium in New York (1927) epitomised this new breed. The 75,000 capacity superstadium had triple-decked stands that wrapped around the field, with an external façade of "imperial symmetry and mass".[9]

5 The majority of cricket grounds, even at the highest level of county cricket in England or interstate cricket in Australia or Sri Lanka have an open ambience. Examples are the International ground at Galle in Sri Lanka, the Adelaide Oval in Australia and the Sussex County Cricket ground in Hove, UK.
6 The first England versus Australia home "Test" match took place at the Oval cricket ground in 1880.
7 The MCG hosted the first cricket match between an English team and Australia in 1862 and the first Test match between the two countries in 1877.

8 BJ Neilson, Dialogue with the City – The Evolution of Baseball Parks, Landscape, 1986.
9 BJ Neilson, ibid

"The idea of the revival of Olympic Games was not a passing fancy: it was the logical culmination of a great movement. The 19th Century saw the taste for physical exercises revive everywhere … At the same time the great inventions, the railways and the telegraph have abridged distances and mankind has come to live a new existence; the peoples have intermingled, they have learned to know each other better and immediately they started to compare themselves. What one achieved the other immediately wished also to endeavour: universal exhibitions brought together to one locality of the globe the products of the most distant lands; literary or scientific congresses have brought together, into contact, the various intellectual forces. How then should the athletes not seek to meet, since rivalry is the basis of athletics, and in reality the very reason of its existence?"

Baron Pierre de Coubertin, 1896

Above: Gustav Klutsis. Design for a postcard for the All-Union Olympiad (Spartakiade), Moscow 1928.

The vision of one man – Baron Pierre de Coubertin – was to revolutionise the significance of stadia. During the celebrations of the fifth anniversary of the Association of the French Athletic Organizations in 1892, he proposed that the ancient Olympic Games be revived, but on a grander scale. In 1894 De Coubertin formed the International Olympic Committee, and the restoration of the Olympic Stadium in Athens was carried out by the architect Metaxas. In 1896, 70,000 spectators packed into the rudimentary stadium for the first Modern Olympic Games, and from there the Olympic Games movement grew. The venues which hosted the early Games were generally unremarkable until, in honour of the founder of the Modern Games, the Olympics were staged in Paris in 1924 at the impressive Stade de Colombes. The 1932 Games were held in the vast reinforced concrete bowl of the Los Angeles Coliseum, and the architectural approach, borrowed directly from Roman precedents, resulted in a stadium which could be seen as a monumental object in the urban landscape: it was the antithesis of the grain and texture of the surrounding suburb. The stadium for the Berlin Olympic Games (1936) was overwhelmingly monumental and gave visible expression to the ambitions of Adolf Hitler. His architect, Werner March, designed a stadium that was intended to symbolise "the permanence, indestructibility and political order of the Third Reich".[10]

Despite the growth and popularity of sport as a form of mass entertainment, the venues – the First Generation of stadia - were large and distinctly uncomfortable places with minimal facilities. Simon Inglis describes a stadium that had "a urinal dug into a bank, whose design might easily have been based on that of a First World War trench".[11] Early pictures of major soccer games show spectators standing on wooden boxes or perched in trees surrounding the venue. Although most of these stadia survived until the 1960s, the arrival of televised sport precipitated an urgent reappraisal of their suitability for the modern game.

10 T Schmidt, Architecture at the Service of Sport: The Olympic Stadium in Los Angeles and Berlin, Olympic Review, No 226, 1986.
11 Simon Inglis, The Football Grounds of Great Britain, Willow Books. London, 1987.

Second Generation Stadia: The Influence of Television

"Television, which had been developed in the 1930s, began broadcasting sports events in the late 1950s. Almost immediately there was a sharp decline in the numbers attending live sporting events. The Second Generation of stadia was the response, placing greater emphasis on the comfort of spectators and improving support facilities in the venue. However, these stadia were still largely concrete bowls and a great many of the world's sporting venues remain as Second Generation stadia".

After the peak crowds of 1950, attendance at soccer games in Britain began to decline. There was general dissatisfaction with the football grounds, which were basically the same 'rotting hulks' of the 1930s. As television coverage grew more sophisticated and stadia facilities remained sub-standard, the novelty of televised images exacerbated the steady decline in the numbers of spectators attending live sports events, and in 1952 the Labour Government's Committee on Copyright announced that broadcasters must compensate sports promoters for their loss of revenue.

The 1960 Olympic Games in Rome were televised and broadcast throughout Europe, and by the early 1960s television was accessible to the majority of the British population, and 27 million viewers watched England beat West Germany in the 1966 Soccer World Cup Final. Television was developing a global reach, and on October 10th 1964, the opening ceremony of the Tokyo Olympic Games was beamed from Japan to North America via the Syncom satellite, making it the world's first trans-Pacific sporting satellite transmission.

Ironically, while television had an adverse impact on the size of sporting crowds, it provided the impetus for improvements to

the ageing stadium structures. Apart from Wembley Stadium, no major soccer stadia had been constructed in Britain for almost 50 years. Ticket sales were the main source of income for football clubs, but ticket revenue alone was insufficient to raise the financial capital for clubs to improve spectator facilities. In the late 1950s legislation threw football clubs a lifeline by permitting them to run their own betting schemes (the pools), which enabled clubs to upgrade their facilities to counter the rising popularity of television. The British Second Generation stadium aimed to entice spectators back to live sport by creating greater comfort with improved seating and with the provision of food and beverage outlets. A full-length cantilevered stand was completed at Sheffield Wednesday's ground at Hillsborough which utilised new building materials, notably aluminium roof sheeting. It was a startling break with the past – an all-seater stand without a paddock in front for standing spectators – and it was mentioned in Nicholas Pevsner's guide to Buildings of England, the only football ground to be so honoured.

Money was also being pumped into stadia redevelopment to ensure that matches would be played despite adverse weather conditions. Floodlighting became a regular feature of baseball and football for night games in the USA in the 1930s, but the English Football Association had banned the use of floodlighting by any of its member clubs in August 1930. The ban was not withdrawn until 1950, and it would be 1967 before every club was equipped with adequate lights.[12] Games could then be played at any time of day, not just on the traditional Saturday afternoon. This new ability to fit in with TV broadcast schedules was significant, but sport did not immediately oust other prime time programmes.

In the 1950s, under-soil heating was introduced, and there were advances made in the understanding of the composition of the playing surface. The scientific study of grass led to the development of various tough varieties, and Kentucky Blue Grass became the surface of choice for baseball and football in the USA. A later development mixed natural grass with polypropylene fibre, which was enhanced by advanced drainage and under-soil heating systems. Astroturf, a plastic synthetic alternative to turf was introduced at the Houston Astrodome in the 1960s when natural grass failed to survive in the internalised environment.

Stadium design in the USA went through a metamorphosis in the 1960s. The automobile and television had revolutionised American lifestyle, and with their newfound mobility, sports fans were not averse to driving out of the city to a stadium located

The 1960s were the television age. Almost everyone could afford a television set, and sport from all over the world could be enjoyed in your own home. Everything seemed possible, the 'global village' was established and conceptually the world began to shrink. Mark McCormack remarked that, "...an unholy alliance was developing. Sport was helping to make television and television was helping to make sport."[16]

Above: Crowd at Wembley Stadium watching Manchester United v Benfica in the 1968 European Cup Final.

on a freeway. Television demanded that stadia be more telegenic, with increased control of the internal environment satisfying a perceived need for predictable playing conditions. Epitomizing the entrepreneurial spirit of Houston, the Astrodome (built in 1965) was the first fully air-conditioned enclosed sports stadium in the world. Comfort was taken to a new level in the Astrodome – giant television screens were erected in the stadium to ensure spectators would not be deprived of the television experience, and it also boasted cushioned seats, five Sky Boxes and a US$2-million electronic scoreboard.[13] In the words of Simon Inglis "It was a building that rejoiced in the possibilities of the age... you didn't have to be an expert to acknowledge that the Astrodome was far ahead of its time."[14]

In Göteborg, Sweden, the Nya Ullevi Stadium (1958) by Fritz Jaenecke and Sten Samuelson was an all-seater stadium with an undulating roof supported by steel cables designed for the 1958 Soccer World Cup. It anticipated changes that would gradually penetrate the British sports scene, along with the radical advances in architecture for the Olympic Games. Pier Luigi Nervi designed the main athletic stadium for the Rome Olympic Games of 1960, but of more interest was the smaller and structurally more innovative Pallazetto della Sport, also by Nervi, whose "devotion to simple geometry and sophisticated prefabrication provided the sports palace with a sublime grace ..."[15] For the 1972 Olympic Games in Munich, Frei Otto (with Gunther Behnisch) designed a spectacular high-tension net of irregular geometry, which supports a transparent plexiglass tented roof extending over the stadium and two adjoining halls.

Television was the saviour of cricket in England, which in the 1960s faced severe financial difficulties with dwindling interest in three-day games and five-day test matches. Often there would be no more than 'three men and a dog' in the ground by the end of an inconclusive county game. In 1965, backed by Rothmans, the BBC put together a package of one-day 40-over games, broadcast live on BBC2 on Sunday afternoons, and this programme revolutionised the game. In 1968, tennis became a professional game when the international controlling bodies permitted Open Championships, which created a resurgence of interest in the televised format.

Third Generation Stadia: The Family Stadium

When Walt Disney launched Disneyland in 1955 (followed by Disney World in 1971), he effectively broke the mould of family entertainment. By creating the theme park, Disney introduced the revolutionary idea that entertainment facilities could attract all the family. Disneyland is, of course, a slightly bizarre experience with its creation of an idealised world of make-believe, a simulacrum of an idealised American town with a city hall, ice-cream parlour, grocery store, schoolroom, county fairground, sheriff's office and white-painted picket fences. Yet it is exactly the place that families could visit for a day out knowing that they would be safe, and that there will be a variety of restaurants and activities.

By contrast all sports were, at that time, predominantly male activities. The journey to the game was an important part of the pre-match ritual and the pre-match camaraderie was part of male bonding – it excluded families and females. But by the mid-1970s, developers and designers were waking up to the idea that if stadia were to effectively compete with theme parks and other leisure facilities, they had to be venues that were not only safe, clean and comfortable, but also where visitors had access to the sort of information they would get through their television at home.

The new stadia had to respond to the challenge of the Disneyworld experience and the concomitant allure of the shopping mall. Walt Disney provided fastidiously clean toilets and a wide range of food outlets, together with four-star hotels and first class public transportation services. The focus was on family entertainment, and sporting venues came under pressure to provide similar amenities. This was the stimulus for the Third Generation of Stadia.

Allied to the provision of better facilities was the need to improve safety. A number of stadium disasters in the 1970s and 1980s sent an urgent signal, to soccer administrators especially, that it was time to improve their safety and security procedures. In 1971, sixty six spectators lost their lives in a stairway crush at the end of a game between Glasgow Rangers and Glasgow Celtic at Ibrox Stadium. Then on May 11th 1985, fire swept through the

---

12 The first floodlit match to involve two league clubs was Carlisle v Darlington, which was played at St. James' Park, Newcastle on 28th November 1955, and the first match played between two 1st Division teams was at Fratton Park between Portsmouth and Newcastle United on 22nd February 1956. By 1956 only 38 of the 92 clubs in the British Football Association had floodlights.
13 The Astrodome has a clear span of 196 metres (642ft), an inside height of 63 metres (208ft), an air-filtering system of activated charcoal, and a man-made field of synthetic grass called Astroturf.

Temperature is a constant 23 degrees centigrade (73 F), with humidity at 50%.
14 Simon Inglis, Sightlines: A Stadium Odyssey, Yellow Jersey Press, London, 2000 pp 263-266.
15 C B Heimsath, Nervi's Methodology, Architecture Forum, February 1960. pp46-48
16 Cited in G Whannell, Fields in Vision: Television, Sport and Cultural Transformation, Routledge, London, 1992.

"When HOK Sport won the Royal Institute of British Architects 'Building of the Year' Award for the Alfred McAlpine Stadium, it was the first sports building to win such an award. Until then sports buildings were simply not regarded as serious architecture in Britain, perhaps in the way that industrial buildings had been treated before Norman Foster changed that perception."

wooden main stand at the Bradford City ground in the north of England. Within five minutes the 76 year old building was an inferno and 56 spectators died in the blaze. Just two weeks later, on the 29th May 1985, a tragedy at the Heysel Stadium in Brussels during the European Cup football final between Liverpool and Juventus claimed 39 lives. The fatalities were partly due to the deplorable condition of the ageing stadium; it was a crumbling 'dinosaur', which had been condemned some years before for failing to meet modern standards. Fighting broke out between rival supporters, and an old wall collapsed when Liverpool fans charged at the Juventus supporters.

Crowd disorder had become a critical problem in the 1970s and 1980s, and while not confined solely to soccer spectators, hooliganism became an unpleasant feature of many national and international soccer matches.[17] Many reasons have been put forward for the growth of violent behaviour at this time: some see it as a response to the commercialisation of the game which had alienated an already deprived socio-economic group from a spectacle that traditionally provided their raison-d'être; and others explain the phenomenon as a code of behaviour from the poorest section of the community, which placed strong emphasis on ties of kinship and territory, male dominance and aggressive expressions of masculinity.[18]

In Britain, the final straw came on 15th April 1989, when 96 Liverpool supporters were killed at the Hillsborough Stadium in Sheffield. It must be stressed that this terrible event was not the result of hooliganism – the police had made the fatal error of opening a gate to allow 4,000 latecomers into the ground, which resulted in hundreds inside being crushed. But it was not just the police who were at fault – the state of the stadium was also criticised. There had been no safety certificate issued for new work undertaken and emergency services could not gain adequate access to the casualties. These incidents reinforced a perception

that a football ground was not the place to take a family. Lord Justice Taylor's report on the Hillsborough deaths, published in January 1990, recommended new safety regulations and the introduction of all-seater stadia. In a relatively short time, it became mandatory for all spectators to be seated at major football games, and this did much to curb the hooligan element associated with many soccer clubs, at least within the grounds.

The Third Generation of stadia emerged in the early 1990s, developing more user-friendly facilities to lure the entire family. Sport was the focus, but not the only attraction, and the principal source of revenue for the sporting clubs changed, shifting from turnstile receipts towards merchandising and television. The Arsenal Football Club and the northern English town of Huddersfield were ahead of the game in the UK. Arsenal built an all-seater stand for 12,500 people at the North Bank end of their Highbury ground, which set a new standard for the quality of spectator facilities, with an abundance of bars, food outlets and supporters' shops. But if Arsenal had set the pace with the quality of new facilities, the Alfred McAlpine Stadium in Huddersfield was to show the way in terms of form.

Opposite: Alfred McAlpine Stadium (now Galpharm Stadium) – Huddersfield, England 1993.

17 There are numerous historical accounts of fighting at Australian cricket games in the mid-19th Century, of crowd problems at American baseball and rioting fans at Canadian ice-hockey games in the 1950s and 1960s. See Kevin Young, Violence and Sport, in Handbook of Sports Studies, SAGE, London, 2000.

18 Kevin Young, "Violence and Sport", in Handbook of Sports Studies, Editors Jay Coakley and Eric Dunning, SAGE, London, 2000

A theoretical 'Stadium of the 1990s' model was proposed in response to the Taylor report. The first opportunity to use this new model for the design of a complete stadium was in a limited competition held for a new venue in Huddersfield. There were five conventional 'box' solutions submitted in the limited architectural competition, in addition to HOK Sport's winning design, which was unlike any stadium seen before in Britain. The dramatic curved forms of the Alfred McAlpine Stadium were the result, and this new model was perfectly timed, as it caught the leading edge of the next major wave in stadium construction in the Britain. From 1994 to 2004 many of the major football clubs built entirely new facilities to provide all-seater accommodation.[19]

The all-seater venue, with its imaginative approach to funding, became the model emulated in several other British cities. The Alfred McAlpine Stadium integrates all of the recommenda-

tions of the Taylor Report. The club's own website touts it as 'The Stadium of the Future'. As well as providing a new home for the Huddersfield soccer and Rugby League teams, the stadium has become a focal point for the town and the surrounding districts. Soon after the Alfred McAlpine Stadium was completed, the all-seater Reebok Stadium was designed for nearby Bolton. The new stadium, completed in 1997, incorporates a museum and an exhibition and conference centre.

The 'Stadium of the 1990s' model was pushed further with the design of Britain's first retractable roofed stadium, the 72,000 seat Millennium Stadium in Cardiff, which was completed for the 1999 Rugby World Cup. Designed as the new Welsh National Stadium, it has already acquired almost religious significance for followers of the national rugby team; a state of mind apparent when the mass singing of Cwm Rhondda or Delilah before a rugby test match threatens to lift the stadium roof off.

19 Other stadia rebuilt in the wake of the Taylor Report were Middlesbrough's BT Cellnet Riverside Stadium (1995), Derby County's Pride Park (1997), Sunderland's Stadium of Light (1997), Wigan Athletic's JJB Stadium (1999) and Southampton's St. Mary's Stadium (2001). In 2002, Leicester City completed the Walker Stadium and Hull City completed the Kingston Communications Stadium. The Huddersfield, Wigan and Hull stadia were unique in Britain in that they accommodated both soccer and rugby league teams.

Above: Reebok Stadium – Bolton, England 1997
Opposite: Millennium Stadium – Cardiff, Wales 1999

Above: Telstra Dome – Melbourne, Australia 2000

Fourth Generation Stadia: Corporate Sponsorship and the Media

"It became clear that stadia could make money if the design, funding and management were integrated. Stadia should not be regarded as a drain on a city's finances. A new era was emerging, of which the new Telstra Dome in Melbourne is a classic example. This is truly a Fourth Generation stadium, with an opening roof, moving seating tiers and a below-pitch car park. This is a blueprint for the city of the future."

If television had been the driving force behind the Second Generation stadia in the 1960s, the money which television could generate in the 1990s acted as the catalyst for further changes in stadium morphology. As Ellis Cashmore notes in Sports Culture, "Jean Baudrillard's work, particularly on the force of electronic media in consumer societies, invites analysis of postmodern sport as owned, controlled, organised and run by mass and multimedia. Baudrillard's image of postmodern society is one in which the media dominate. Consumption is the central mode of postmodern existence and sport is now subject to the kinds of critical appraisal associated with other areas of social life."[20] Digital television, satellite communications and the internet are the main factors driving the Fourth Generation stadium model.

The Fourth Generation stadium is a direct result of the demands of satellite TV. Events are marketed so that a 90-minute soccer game or an 80-minute rugby international game becomes a programme in itself, with replays, commentary, punditry and after-match criticism. Baseball with its 'innings' and American football with its distinct 'quarters' are perfectly suited for TV, and the games themselves have adapted to meet the demands of TV channels. 'Time outs' are taken in American football games solely for advertising purposes.

At the beginning of the 21st Century, satellite TV and sport have developed an appreciable degree of interdependence. Developments in satellite technology and digital recording have combined to produce spectacular entertainment on screen, and surprisingly it appears that attendance has not been adversely affected. The increasing amount of live football on British television has actually been paralleled by a steady growth in match attendances over the last 10 years. A sports event is now regarded as a communal activity with certain rituals, and this cannot be replicated or replaced by the televised product, even when it is experienced in a public place such as a bar or a pub.

Sport is increasingly a commercial commodity, and since the banning of tobacco advertising, sports governing bodies have relied on the sale of television rights. Ted Turner and Rupert Murdoch have been the central figures in the worldwide transformation of televised sport. Between 1983 and 1991, the annual TV rights income for UK soccer rose from £2.6 million to £11 million, but in 1992 Rupert Murdoch's BSkyB entered the bidding, and the income jumped to £38.3 million per annum. In 1997 the company again secured the broadcasting rights, this time for £168 million per annum and in 2001 BSkyB paid £367 million per annum. The Fox Entertainment Group Inc (owned by Rupert Murdoch's News Corp) paid US$350 million in the late 1990s for the Los Angeles Dodgers, and Ted Turner, then with AOL Time Warner acquired the Atlantic Braves.[21] This ensured both owners had a voice in the scheduling of baseball games. AOL Time Warner also has a financial interest in the Atlantic Hawks and the Thrashers; Disney owns ESPN, the Anaheim Angels and the Chicago Cubs, and Cablevision has a controlling interest in the New York Knicks and the New York Rangers. Ted Turner's concept of the Goodwill Games transformed athletics into a lucrative global sport, and the Australian media giant Kerry Packer did the same for cricket.

20 Ellis Cashmore, Sports Culture: An A-Z Guide, Routledge, London, 2000. p280.
21 The Fox Entertainment Group sold the LA Dodgers to Frank McCourt on January 29th 2004 for US$ 430 million. Ted Turner quit his post as Vice Chairman of AOL Time Warner in February 2003. The company still own the Atlantic Braves and their stadium retains the name Turner Field.

Satellite television has placed great demands on Fourth Generation stadia designers. The stadium is the 'backdrop' to the televised performance and optimum lighting levels are required for high resolution colour transmissions.[22] With these lighting standards in place, games can be played at any time, day or night, and most significantly, they can then be slotted into highly remunerative global TV schedules. The on-screen image of a stadium is crucial to television coverage, as a packed 40,000 seat stadium has much more atmosphere than an 80,000 seat stadium which is half full. Acoustic considerations and the acknowledgement of spectator participation have now become key design factors. In a curious way, sport has come full circle. The spectators and players were cheek by jowl in First Generation venues, but the multi-use stadia pushed the spectator away from the playing field, separated by the obligatory athletic track. Now we see the desire to directly re-engage the spectators with the sport.

A watershed was the 1984 Los Angeles Olympic Games, when the organising committee successfully negotiated a series of unprecedented marketing partnerships with corporations such as American Express and Anheuser Busch. The Olympic logo appeared on packaged products and the Games yielded a profit of US$225 million. This was the first time corporate sponsorship of the Games had been permitted, and 43 companies used the Olympic rings for advertising. A legacy of the Los Angeles Olympics was the sports marketing industry, when corporate marketers began to move dollars from traditional advertising into event driven expenditure. The corporate world embraced sports marketing, and consequently the imperative to provide improved stadium amenities became apparent. Corporate sponsors and the provision of corporate hospitality boxes became a necessity in the financing of new stadia, and although individual seat sales remained a substantial source of revenue, a large part of a stadium's revenue now came from the sale of corporate facilities.

"Stadia have come of age. They have grown into buildings that can be used as catalysts for the planned and strategic growth of 21st Century cities. Stadia have become powerful symbols of our culture, our aspirations and, sometimes, of our failures. We need to learn how to use them wisely, and how to get the most out of their potential."

Fifth Generation Stadia: Urban Regeneration

Each generation of stadia has 'raised the bar', adding a new level of sophistication and improved facilities. Now, at the beginning of the 21st Century, a new potential has emerged; the ability of stadia to shape new cities and to regenerate decaying areas of old cities. The stadium typology can provide all the elements required to achieve a critical mass capable of sustaining city life: a critical mass containing the residential, commercial, retail, leisure and transport components which encourage cities to thrive. Inner city stadium construction during the last decade has revitalized the cities of Baltimore, Denver, Cincinnati, Pittsburgh, Cardiff, Melbourne, Brisbane, Lisbon and San Francisco.

The crucial determinants for stadium design in the 21st Century will be the potential for urban regeneration, and the role of the 'iconic' stadium in the marketing and positioning of a global city. The Fifth Generation stadium is a less tangible piece of architecture than the previous four generations, it will be identified and categorized by its global presence and by its regional regenerative potential.

22 Many floodlighting schemes have a skeletal lighting tower positioned at each of the four corners of the pitch. The Alfred McAlpine Stadium, the Faro/Loule Stadium, and the Westpac Stadium are prime examples. But several recent designs have the principal floodlights located below the lip of the stadium roof in order that there should not be excessive spillover of light to adjoining residential areas. This applies in the case of the Suncorp Stadium, Estádio da Luz and Arsenal's new Emirates Stadium.

Above: Heinz Field – Pittsburgh, Pennsylvania, USA 2001

Reebok Stadium
Bolton, England
1997

"The Reebok Stadium forms
a dramatic and optimistic
edge to the largely depressed
Bolton conurbation. Built
on a former refuse tip, the
stadium signals regeneration
as effectively as any town-
centre facelift. Like the new
stadium in Huddersfield,
which is Bolton's immediate
precursor, bold and unre-
strained structural expression
gives the Reebok a presence
which defines its relatively
small size."

Professor Brian Edwards, University of
Huddersfield. From an appraisal in
"Premier League", The Architects'
Journal, 22 January, 1998.

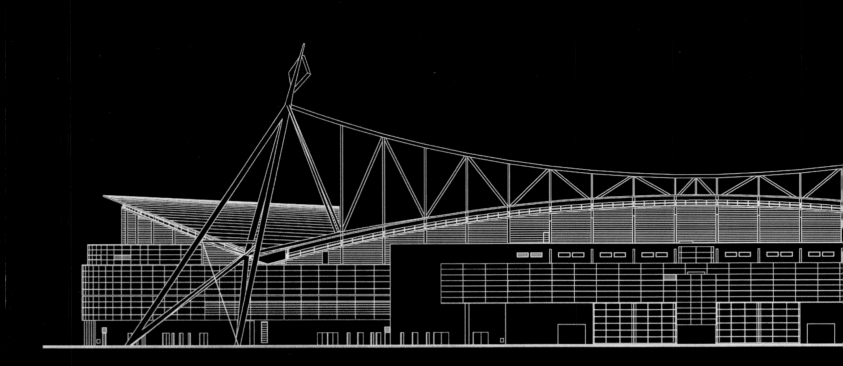
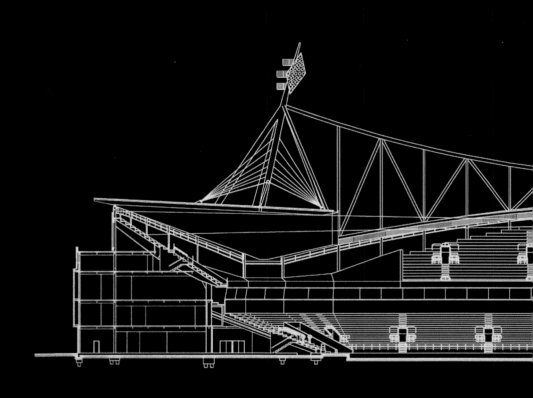

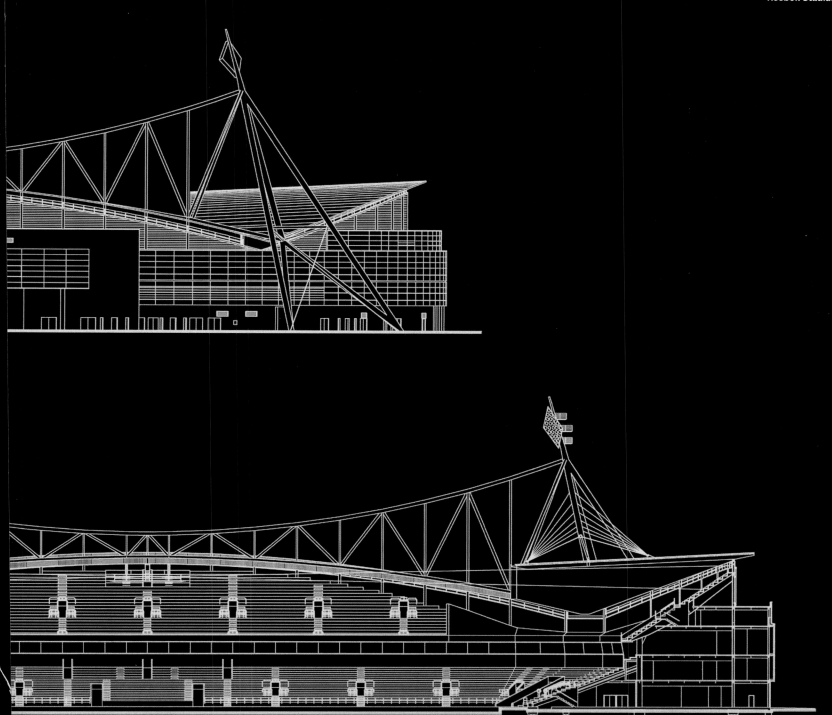

121

"If, like me, you are one of those poor souls who delights at the mere glimpse of floodlights on the horizon, try driving along the M61 motorway in north west England. Set back from the road is an extraordinary sight - the 25,000 seat Reebok Stadium, home to Bolton Wanderers. Like a giant cat's cradle of white steel, with diamond shape floodlights angled over the bowl, the structure is unlike any traditional football ground. And yet its function is immediately recognisable."

Simon Inglis, September 2001. From British Council website: footballculture.net

122

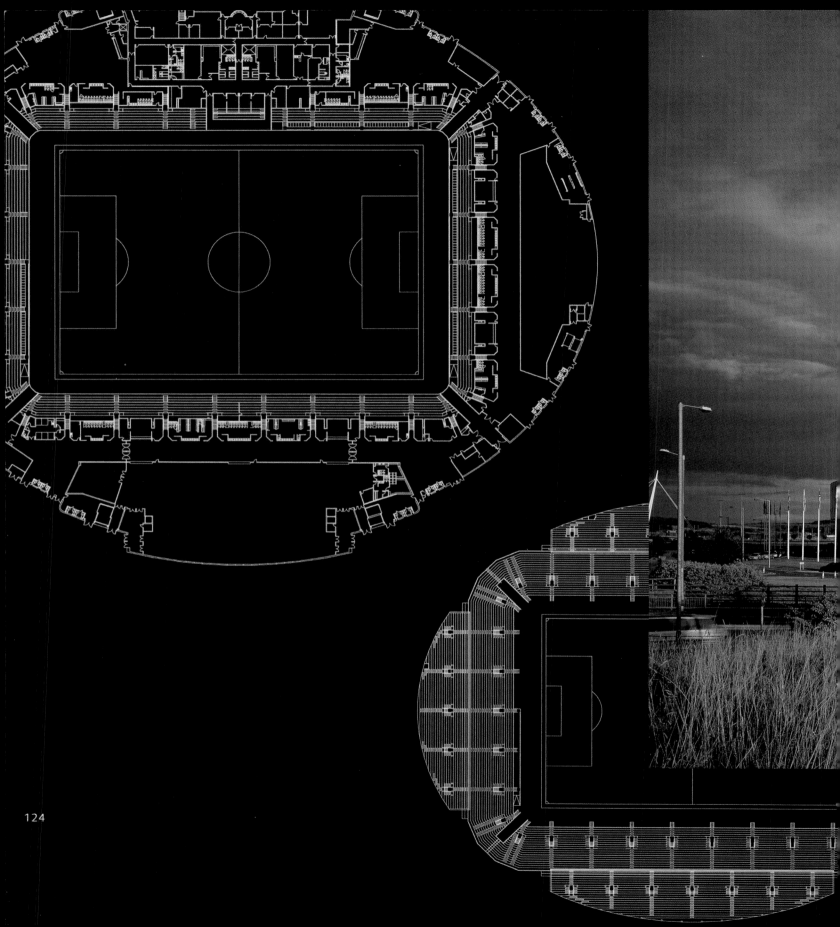

The flexibility of the original design has enabled the incremental accommodation of further developments, without compromising the aesthetic harmony of the structure. A De Vere Whites hotel has now been integrated on the eastern side of Reebok Stadium, and 19 of the 125 rooms have views of the pitch.

126

The form of the Reebok Stadium is dominated by the graphic roof structure, which sails over a clearly articulated bowl. The roof consists of four leaning and tapering tubular steel towers, each providing support for the main steel roof trusses, which span the full length of the pitch, parallel to the touchline and across both ends. The curved trusses taper towards the centre of the span, the roof covering appears as a continuous scalloped canopy and the floodlighting towers were designed as an integral part of the steel structure.

The roof was the most visible sign of the dramatic changes taking place in stadium architecture and planning during the 1990s. Whether seen as a symbol, read as a metaphor or simply admired for its inherent beauty, the roof of a stadium cannot be ignored. Advanced computer software enabled structural gymnastics: made tangible with materials such as PTFE, profiled steel, laminated plexiglass and translucent polycarbonate. Exhilarating forms and spaces are now standard design tools.

SBC Park

(formerly Pacific Bell Park)

San Francisco, California, USA

2000

The design of SBC Park was largely directed by the desire for a traditional ballpark in a wonderful Bayside location; it was to be a place where "Wrigley Field meets Camden Yards". The two street-facing façades embrace the local context: the brick and stone podium is rusticated, with quoins at the corners and recesses, a dado wall is introduced and a setback occurs at the 3rd storey roof level where the structure changes to steel, reflecting the industrial image of the harbour and warehouse. It picks up on the language of the city's early 20th Century industrial legacy and the four storey brownstone apartments along the Embarcadero. Plazas, two clock towers and stands of palm trees mediate between the stadium and its context – softening the edge. The expressed steel structure of the upper levels complements the Lefty O'Doul Bridge (seen to the right), a bascule type drawbridge listed on the National Historic Properties Register.

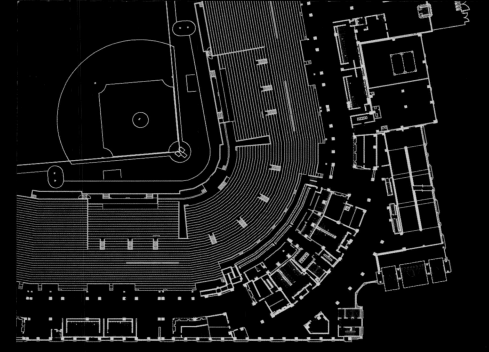

"Sittin' in the morning sun
I'll be sittin' when the evenin' come
Watching the ships roll in
And then I watch 'em roll away again

I'm sittin' on the dock of the bay
Watching the tide roll away
I'm just sittin' on the dock of the bay
Wastin' time

I left my home in Georgia
Headed for the 'Frisco Bay
'Cause I had nothing to live for
And look like nothin's gonna come my way

So I'm just gonna sit on the dock of the bay
Watching the tide roll away
I'm sittin' on the dock of the bay
Wastin' time"

From '(Sittin' on) The Dock of the Bay'
by Otis Redding and Steve Cropper, 1968.

SBC Park was intended as an urban ballpark, a neighbourhood ballpark, a ballpark that recalls the history of baseball and one that embraces the city of San Francisco. Wind studies determined the direction of the stadium, which was originally intended to face the city skyline, and it now faces the Oakland Bay Bridge, with wonderful views to the Oakland Hills over the yacht harbour and the San Francisco Bay. The capacity of the stadium is 41,503 – a figure inflated by the non-paying members of the 'knothole gang', who make use of the standing room in the arches along the waterfront – reviving memories of old ballparks surrounded by wooden fences, with knotholes providing free views of the game. Home runs fly into the Bay over the heads of the 'knothole gang', and a flotilla of waiting boats scramble to souvenir the balls.

This intrinsic awakening of community spirit has revitalized San Francisco's old warehouse district, and SBC Park is now the linchpin of the massive regeneration of the Mission Bay area to the south, currently a forlorn wasteland of abandoned railyards and parking lots.

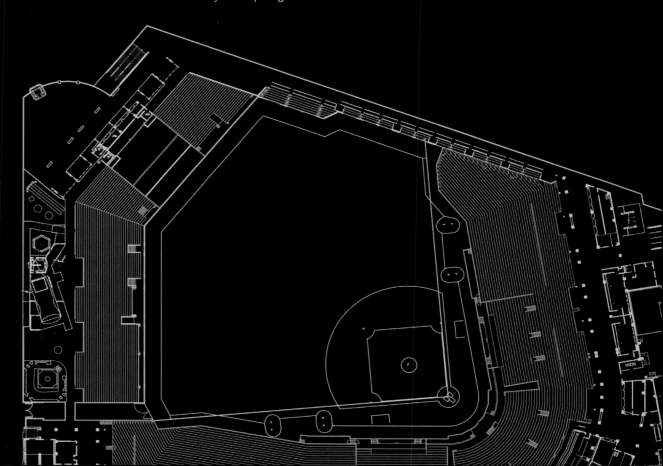

Westpac Stadium

Wellington, New Zealand

2000

Sited on disused railway yards on the edge of Wellington Harbour, the 34,500 seat Westpac Stadium is the world's first modern purpose-built cricket ground. The oval shape of the stadium has also worked very well for rugby, New Zealand's most popular sport. The design demonstrates a minimalist approach, with the cricket arena cut back to the tightest possible configuration, allowing the stadium to accommodate rugby games without placing the spectators too far from the pitch.

The building's external skin of horizontally-striated, reflective metal cladding has created a large sculptural landmark on the northern edge of the central business district. The roof is not the dominant feature, and the lighting masts appear as delicate protrusions emerging from the pure geometric form. The stadium's single-tier continuous seating produces a sense of enclosure and intensity. Elevated corporate boxes are slung beneath the roof structure, contributing to the stadium's intimidating atmosphere.

134

Westpac Stadium (formerly WestpacTrust Stadium) was designed by an HOK Sport + Venue +Event joint venture, Bligh Lobb Sports Architecture in association with Architecture Warren and Mahoney.

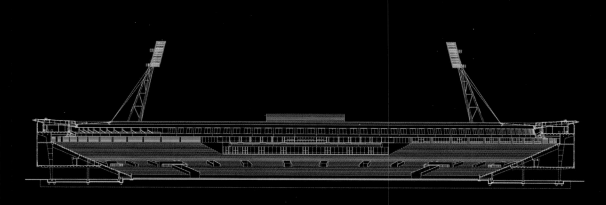

"The effect on the popularity of rugby has been amazing. Our season ticket holders increased from 1,000 at Athletic Park in 1999 to 14,000 – this is our limit – at the stadium and there is already a waiting list of 3,000. And in total this year, we have had 346,000 people attend rugby events at the new stadium.

In 2000, the Wellington Lions National Provincial Championship team attracted 151,000 people for their five home games. That equates to an average of 30,000 people per game for the Lions. Our average at Athletic Park in 1999 was 12,000 people per game. Needless to say, we're thrilled with those results. They just go to show what a new stadium can do for a sport."

Brett Jackson, of the Wellington Rugby Football Union. 2 November, 2000.

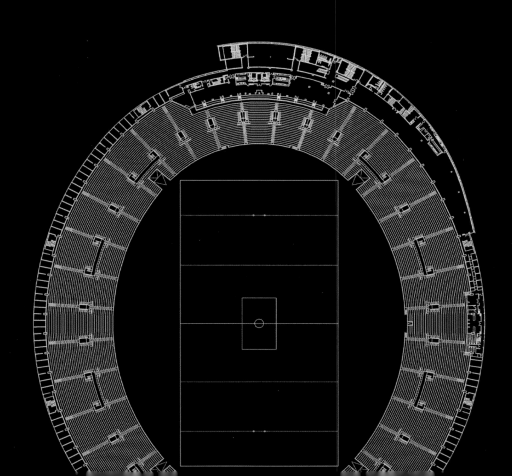

137

Telstra Dome

(formerly Colonial Stadium)

Melbourne, Australia

2000

"Stadia, along with churches, are the structures designed to bring our communities together. There is no other opportunity these days to be part of such a crowd: the Mexican Wave and the songs we sing with a thousand strangers link us with a greater group; we are part of a whole and we are part of something special. And most importantly, we are there to experience that moment in time. However these buildings called 'stadia' are often dull and uninteresting places: no more than concrete bowls, lacking basic amenities, and so bleak and unfriendly as to be frightening; more obsessed with the head counts at the turnstiles than with the heartbeats of the experience.

Telstra Dome is different: it is a true sporting 'church' of our time. The spirit, the camaraderie and the atmosphere of a great sporting event are enhanced by a great stadium. The venue is not a passive backdrop, but a set which intensifies the drama of the occasion."

Rod Sheard

Telstra Dome, formerly Colonial Stadium, was designed by an HOK Sport joint venture, Bligh Lobb Sports Architecture and Daryl Jackson Pty Ltd. HOK Sport + Venue + Event is an HOK Sport subsidiary.

"It's just an outstanding place to play. When I first started playing, if someone had said to me that I was a chance at playing a Test match under a roof in an enclosed stadium, I would have thought they were crazy.

As everyone saw there tonight, the atmosphere is just quite incredible. It is just a great way and place to play rugby."

John Eales, Australian rugby union captain, quoted in The Sunday Age, 8 July, 2001.

"Stadia are entertainment buildings, a building type largely ignored by city planners over the last 25 years. That is understandable: the earlier versions were usually dull to look at – low budget and low art solutions. That has all changed in the 21st Century – they are now high budget and high art public buildings. They contribute intrinsically to urban areas and can totally transform a community. They create precincts where people gather to enjoy themselves, and the representation of that 'enjoyment' is a new concept in architecture."

Rod Sheard

The 53,000 seat Telstra Dome is an
urban stadium: it is a landmark for the
city of Melbourne and a catalyst for
the regeneration of the Docklands
area to the city's west. As the
Docklands redevelopment continues
over the next twenty years, Telstra
Dome will be at the centre of
Melbourne's expanded inner city.

The design of the stadium broke
the mould with its combination of
advanced technology, digital capability
and multifunctionality. A retractable
roof and moving seating tiers were
used for the first time in an Australian
stadium. The retractable roof has been
a major breakthrough in the siting of
a city stadium, as it contains light and
noise breakout, as well as improving
spectator comfort and creating atmosphere. The moving tiers of seats
mean that the arena can be used for
Australian rules and cricket (played on
an oval), but the crowd is brought 18
metres closer to a rectangular pitch for
soccer and rugby. Some spectators
can have 'smart seats', which have a
video replay monitor fitted into the
extended arm of the seats, showing
instant replays, player profiles and...
movies.

145

Estádio Algarve

Faro/Loulé, Portugal

2004

The 30,000 seat Estádio Algarve has an appropriate profile for a stadium located on the southern Atlantic coast. The form and structural expression of the stadium is symbolic of the nautical traditions of Faro and the great maritime history of Portugal. The crustacean-like roofs, with fabric in scalloped sections stretched over the steel frame, also make reference to the fishing industry of the Iberian peninsular.

Estádio Algarve sits in a natural amphitheatre below olive-tree clad hills with a distant view of the ocean. The stadium is the first stage of the Parques das Cidades, a new development undertaken by both the municipalities of Faro and Loulé. Initially built for the Euro 2004 Championships, the stadium was designed to integrate with the local environment and landscape as well as the overall masterplan for the Parque das Cidades. It will be used for concerts and large community events as well as football matches.

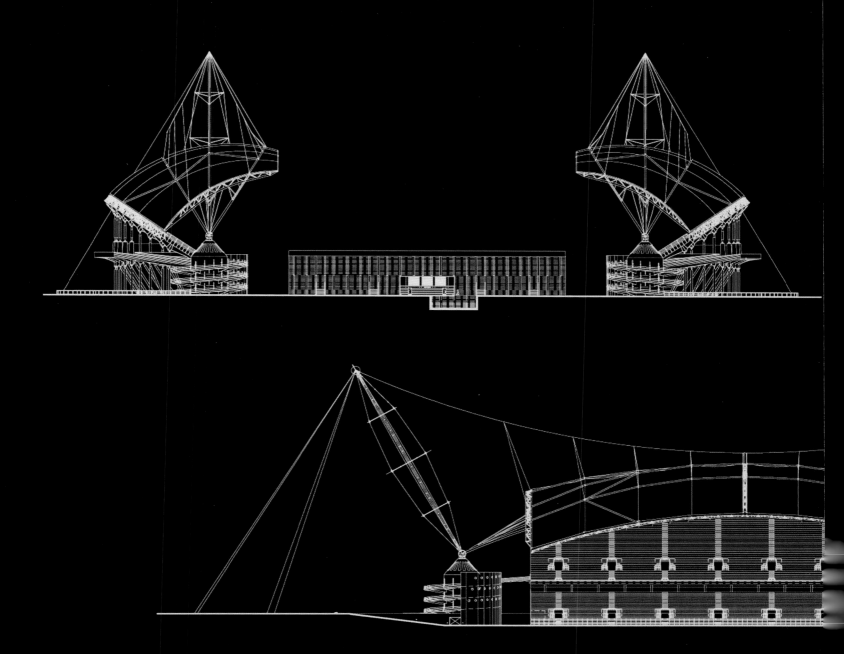

150   The design of the stadium was a sustainable response to the context of the Algarve region of southern Portugal. The billowing fabric roof and the spiral ramps, both in their forms and with their use of materials, evoke the traditions of rural and maritime architecture in the Algarve. The aggregate used for the stadium's concrete was from the *calcario* stone excavated on site, and a landscape of tree-lined paths and gardens will blend with the surrounding hills of olive trees and fields of vines.

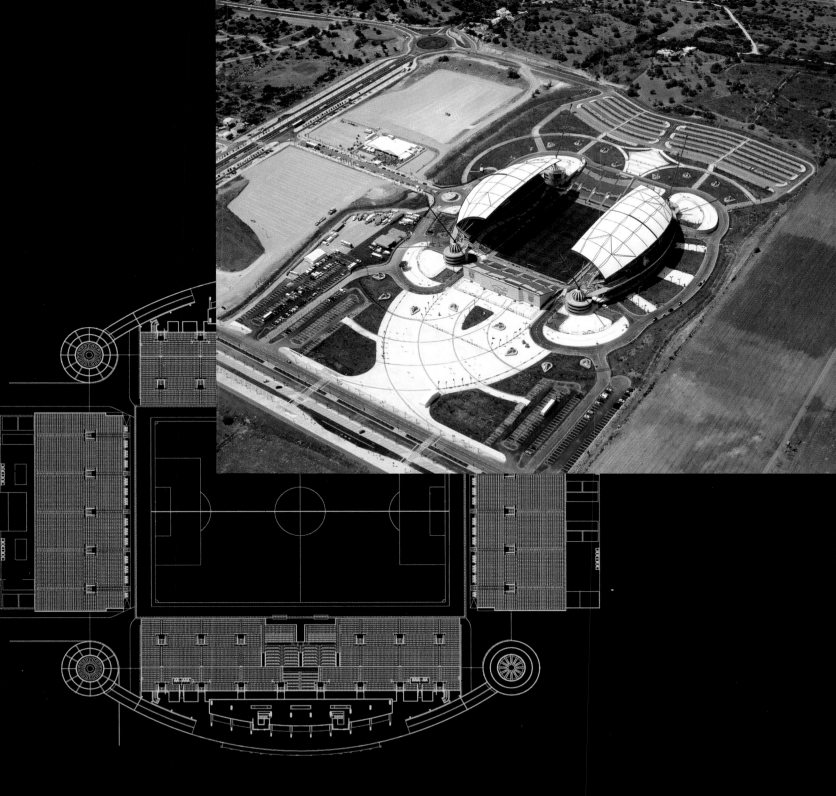

The inspiration for the patterns of paving and retaining walls in the surrounding
Parques des Cidades came from the surrounding topography. Lines of stone
paviors radiate outwards, reminiscent of Michelangelo's Piazza del Campidoglio
and the Baroque curves of traditional Portuguese architecture.

153

The Stadium and the City

"The stadium is a complex planning tool. If it is used wisely, it can help a city grow, especially on barren sites. A great deal of regeneration in cities takes place in an understated unglamorous way, with people quietly moving into refurbished buildings. This is the type of city regeneration for which a sporting venue can act as a catalyst.

This regeneration will occur increasingly, due to the 'emotional' acceptance of an area when it is used for sport. People see the area in a very different light. There is an 'atmosphere' created around a sporting event, which generates powerful and intense emotions. The emotional experience of attending and participating in a major sporting event is exhilarating. It is not just the event, there is an 'afterglow' and this illuminates the whole area."

Above: Great American Ballpark – Cincinnati, Ohio, USA 2003

In the period after World War II, most European cities faced severe problems of overcrowding, and the immediate solution was seen to be the decentralisation of population. The British New Towns Act of 1946 led to the creation of 30 new towns, and between 1947 and 1970 the decaying inner city areas of London, Liverpool, Glasgow and Tyneside were cleared and a large proportion of the population moved to the periphery. There was a similar flight to the suburbs in North America. Industry followed suit, with the relocation of factories to 'greenfield' sites in more accessible locations. But politicians and planners became increasingly alarmed at the subsequent phenomenon of large areas of inner cities being left derelict, with nothing replacing their economic base. Jane Jacobs' seminal book The Death and Life of Great American Cities (1965) highlighted many of the looming problems.[1]

By the end of the 1980s, many cities in the Western world were in a state of crisis, and global economic restructuring compounded the problems already in place. Established manufacturing industries were dying out in the face of competition from the emerging economies of Asia, and new technology in the field of transportation made waterfront warehouses and railheads redundant. As the cities decentralised, the inner cores were abandoned to the poor and to minorities.[2] Where 'urban renewal' and 'comprehensive redevelopment' did take place, it was usually in the form of large-scale corporate office towers in zoned areas, accessed by freeways which carved through the inner urban core.[3] Between 1960 and 1985, all the docks of London (the largest port in Britain) were closed, as containerization took over shipping and the port facilities moved downstream to Tilbury, Felixstowe and over the channel to Rotterdam. Steelmaking, shipbuilding, mining, textile production and automobile manufacturing all suffered a similar fate in other cities, accelerated by government policy which gave market forces a free rein to produce 'a leaner fitter industry'. London's docklands were decimated, and the scenario was repeated in European cities such as Barcelona, Bilbao and Genoa. Cities that had built their wealth on rail transportation suffered as containerized loads were switched to road transport. In the USA, the railheads in Baltimore were run down, the steelworks in Pittsburgh became redundant and the dockyards in San Francisco were vacated. The Victoria Docks, which had been Melbourne's key port until the 1960s, fell into disuse when cargo shifted to containers.

The phrase 'Rust Belt' was used, often derisively, to refer to cities in the traditional industrial heartlands of the American Mid West, the Ruhr Valley, Northern England and Scotland. The word 'regeneration' entered the language of politicians and sociologists, and planners and architects saw the wasteland of the urban core as the new frontier. 'Regeneration' is defined as 'the regrowth of an organ, or a tissue that has been injured…" and alludes to "spiritual renewal…." And in this context, it was seen as a holistic process aimed at re-populating the inner cities, repairing the physical fabric, renewing economic structures and reviving social life.

The 1992 United Nations Rio Summit on the Environment brought regeneration to the fore with its focus on global issues.

1 Jane Jacobs, The Death and Life of Great American Cities, Harmondsworth, Penguin, 1965.
2 Roberta Brandes Gratz with Norman Mitz, Cities - Back from the Edge – New Life for Downtown, John Wiley & Sons Inc, 1988.
3 Steven Litt, Urbanism of the Reagan Era, Urban Design Quarterly, Issue 34, April 1990, pp 3-5.

"Today, major sporting facilities are a mainstay of urban regeneration and their potential has been recognised. However, a stadium alone will not transform a blighted area, it must be part of an overall plan to attract commercial, retail and recreational activities; and, most importantly, people. The stadium must integrate with a neighbourhood, a district or a city."

There was a concerted movement to address areas devastated by economic and social decline, the so-called 'brownfield' sites of rusting railway yards, decaying industrial sheds, redundant dock-yards and chemically polluted landscapes. This was the detritus of countries undergoing transition to a knowledge-based society. A 1999 report by Richard Rogers to the London Urban Task Force, entitled Towards an Urban Renaissance, emphasised that regeneration has to be design led.[4] Regeneration inevitably requires an economic catalyst, and in the 1990s it became apparent that stadia were capable of fulfilling this role.

Baltimore's Oriole Park at Camden Yards saw the integration of a baseball stadium into the wider urban plan for the rebirth of a city. The area adjacent to the inner harbour was already showing signs of life as a result of the city's 20-year economic development strategy, but Oriole Park was pivotal in the area's successful regeneration. The stadium was sited to anchor the southern end of the waterfront renewal, and this effectively turned the derelict Camden Yards B&O railhead into an extension of an entertainment and tourist centre, creating a landmark for destination marketing. A large historic transit warehouse, which formerly served the railway company, has been retained as an integral part of the ballpark, creating a unique backdrop. Ticket offices, restaurants and retail facilities are housed in the former warehouse.

The economic impact of Oriole Park validates the potential of stadia to generate tourism, with 1.6 million baseball fans coming from outside the city every year to watch games, with many staying overnight in the Baltimore area. The dollars spent inside Oriole Park and in nearby hotels, restaurants, gas stations and retail outlets reverberate through the local economy with a 'multiplier effect', typically five or six times the original level of

4 Richard Rogers (Chairman), Urban Task Force, Towards an Urban Renaissance, Department of the Environment, Transport and the Regions, E & FN Spon, London, 1999.

Above and opposite: Oriole Park at Camden Yards – Baltimore, Maryland, USA 1992

159

160   Above: Coors Field – Denver, Colorado, USA 1995

spending. In their first three seasons at Camden Yards, the Baltimore Orioles averaged 45,442 spectators per game, and more than 40% of spectators heading for the ball game combined it with a business or pleasure trip.

Oriole Park symbolizes the regeneration of Baltimore's inner harbour and downtown areas, and it provides a focus for the emotions and aspirations of the wider community. The Camden Yards redevelopment has helped revitalise a rundown area of Baltimore, "that not long ago scared the life out of timid suburbanites".[5]

Coors Field, home of the Colorado Rockies, was completed in 1995 and has been the catalyst for the regeneration of a downtown area of Denver, known colloquially as the LoDo. Little more than a decade ago the LoDo was in downward spiral of decline, an area where drive-by police patrols would warn visitors to stay off the street at night. A pedestrian mall, a collection of high-end retailers and art galleries have followed the opening of the baseball stadium, and the LoDo now has the largest concentration of restored turn-of-the-century buildings in the USA, with 26 blocks containing late 19th Century brick warehouses. The success of Coors Field paved the way for the Pepsi Centre (home of the Colorado Avalanche hockey team and Denver Nuggets basketball team), and other large retail, residential and entertainment projects.

In 1995, the San Francisco Giants announced plans for the first privately financed Major League ballpark to be built in more than 30 years.[6] The ballpark is located on a 5.25-hectare waterfront site at China Basin, and it has revived a previously rundown area. SBC Park (then known as Pacific Bell Park) was completed in 2000, and sparked off a flurry of residential development in the neighbouring old warehouse district. SBC Park is the northern anchor of a much larger regeneration project that extends south into Mission Bay between the elevated 280 Freeway and San

Francisco Bay. The area is currently a desolate mixture of parking lots, torn up streets, a few remaining warehouses and abandoned railyards, but the first of a planned 6,000 residential units are taking shape employing New Urbanist guidelines. Within a generation, it is anticipated that this will be a leafy mixed-use neighbourhood, wrapped around a University of California-San Francisco campus and traversed by a Muni light rail line. The first phase of the redevelopment is currently under construction between SBC Park and the Caltrain Depot on King Street.

'Fifth Generation stadia are not 'stand-alone' buildings; they should be seen as dynamic cells implanted into the urban fabric of a city, stimulating growth and inspiring regeneration.'

5 Tom Farrey, The Seattle Times, 20th August 1995.
6 The San Francisco Giants have enjoyed a long association with the city of San Francisco but in 1992 owner Bob Lurie was on the point of selling the team. In January 1993, Peter Magowan moved quickly to purchase the Giants and consequently to keep the franchise and the team in San Francisco. Magowan, who led a group of San Francisco business leaders always knew the Giants franchise was not secure in San Francisco until a new ballpark was built to replace the ageing Candlestick Park venue.

Above: SBC Park – San Francisco, California, USA 2000

"The urban design principles driving the planning of Heinz Field and PNC Park have been instrumental in the reinvention of the city of Pittsburgh. The construction of the stadia, together with the associated retail, leisure, residential and commercial developments, represents a new philosophy that redefines what 'Downtown' is all about. It becomes an integrated place of working, living, gathering and celebrating – a comprehensive experience that ultimately symbolises Pittsburgh."

In 1880, Pittsburgh was the "hearth of the nation" and remained so for much of the 20th Century, with "smokestacks lined against the fiery red night sky, the curving rivers with their steel-girdered bridges, [and] the blazing furnaces".[7] The steel mills and foundries departed with the economic upheavals of the 1970s, leaving behind a dismal post-industrial landscape. The Pittsburgh city planners are now in the process of developing a major urban plan extending over several city blocks surrounding Heinz Field Stadium and the adjoining PNC Baseball Park. The construction of the two new stadia, integrated with retail, leisure, residential and commercial development has led to a reassessment of the concept of 'downtown'. The PNC Ballpark has generated a 6.5-hectare (16 acre) development including a public river walk, an outdoor amphitheatre and a low-density retail, office and residential development.

A stadium can also act as the catalyst for structured growth of sprawling metropolitan areas. The major venues for the 2000 Olympic Games were located on one site, at the demographic centre of Greater Sydney, 17 kilometres west of the CBD. The Games organisers faced considerable criticism for not following the Barcelona model, which selected sites scattered throughout

Above: PNC Park – Pittsburgh, Pennsylvania, USA 2001

7 Spiro Kostov, The City Shaped, Thames and Hudson, London. 1991. p282.

Above: Heinz Field – Pittsburgh, Pennsylvania, USA 2001

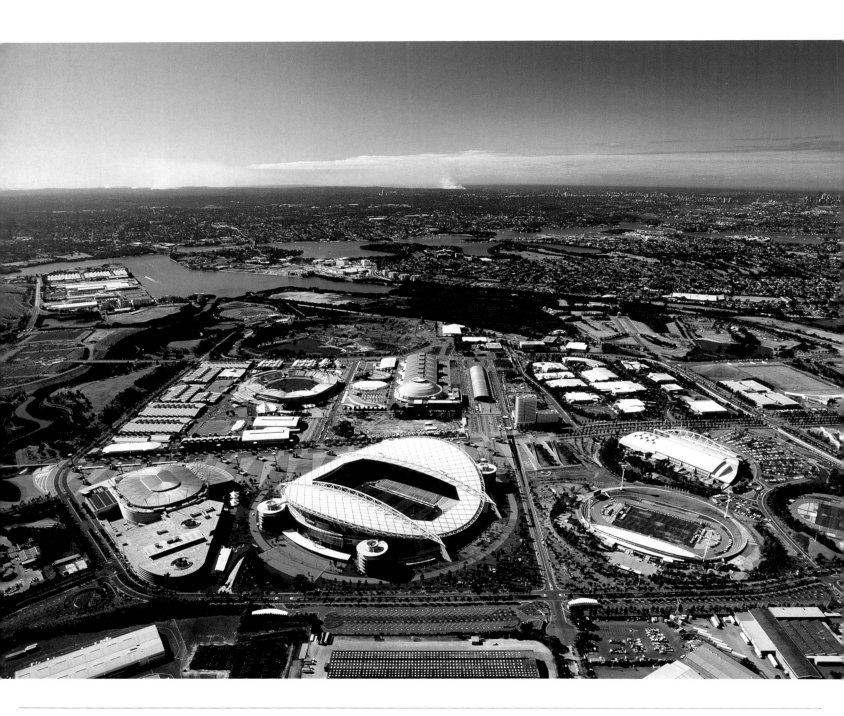

Above: Telstra Stadium (formerly Stadium Australia) and 2000 Olympic
Games site – Sydney, Australia

"Cities have always been places to work, and it is now understood that they also need to be places to live, if we do not want them to die in the evening. Fifth Generation stadia recognise that living and working are not the complete picture: our city centres require entertainment, celebration and drama."

the metropolis, reinvigorating the entire urban tissue. Sydney chose instead to create a new focus for the metropolitan region on a neglected area, which had at various times been an industrial site, a brickworks, an abattoir, an armaments store and a highly polluted refuse dump. But Homebush Bay was an accessible site, located near major road, rail and ferry links, and the completed project saw the hugely successful reclamation of a massive area. It offered the potential for Sydney to establish a focal point west of the city centre, and utilised the sporting complex and surrounding parklands as a stimulus for new residential development.

Telstra Dome (formerly Colonial Stadium) has driven the redevelopment and economic resurgence of Melbourne's former docklands, including seven kilometres of waterfront, on the western edge of the city's CBD. Likewise, Brisbane's Suncorp Stadium forms one of the principal features and landmarks of the City West urban regeneration plan, which aims to link the educational, sporting, cultural and residential precincts of the inner west suburbs to the Brisbane CBD. Other key projects in the revitalisation of western Brisbane include the new Roma Street Parklands, Southbank and the refurbished Queensland Cultural Centre. Associated regeneration has taken place, with local restaurant and cafe owners upgrading and rebranding for the opening of the stadium in 2003. The next stage of the area's regeneration includes the future development of Roma Street Railyards, a direct western entry to the CBD from a Roma Street/Milton Road Boulevard and an extension of the public domain through the barracks precinct at Petrie Terrace.

The 1992 Olympic Games in Barcelona provided the stimulus required for that city to spruce up its public spaces, to clean up its beaches and, most importantly, to reconnect the city with the sea. The city fabric is now so thoroughly transformed that it is difficult to recall the beautiful, but shabby and rundown city of the 1970s. The Olympic Games did not mark the end of the transformation process, and in the following decade new plazas and parks opened up old parts of the city, the markets were rejuvenated and the public realm has been enhanced. So completely has this change been effected that Peter Buchanan suggests that Barcelona, which affirms the interdependency of home, work and leisure, might be a model for the post-industrial city.[8]

In the 1960s, the Estádio da Luz, home of Benfica Football

8 Peter Buchanan, Barcelona: a city regenerated, Architectural Review, No. 1146, London, August 1992, p11/8

Above: Telstra Dome (formerly Colonial Stadium) – Melbourne, Australia 2000

Club and graced by the subtle skills of Eusebio, was the largest stadium in Europe. Located in a working class neighbourhood of Lisbon, it was affectionately referred to as 'The Cathedral'.[9] However by the late 1990s, the 50-year-old structure was showing signs of age and it was clear that if it was to stage the Euro 2004 soccer championships, it would have to be rebuilt on an adjoining site. The new stadium, built for the 2004 championships, is leading the rebirth of the Luz district. Portugal's largest hypermarket adjoins the stadium, which itself includes facilities for volleyball, basketball, indoor soccer and boxing, with an Adidas Mega Store. The surrounding area has been landscaped as a park and a huge plaza, creating a newly configured spiritual home for the supporters of Portugal's most loved football team

The rebuilding and upgrading of the ten stadia in Portugal as venues for Euro 2004 was accompanied by the building of new infrastructure, which included the upgrading of motorways, airports and railways. Likewise, Greece utilized the 2004 Olympic Games to implement the upgrading of dilapidated buildings, and neglected streets and pavements. New metro lines, a new tram system, 130 kilometres of highway and 10,000 hectares of tree planting were put in place in preparation for the Games, and the restoration of the Acropolis became a priority.[10] Cardiff, the capital city of Wales, was one of the world's leading coal ports at the turn of the century, but with the closure of many mines in South Wales in the 1920s and further closures in the 1960s, the docks were redundant and the dockland area derelict. By the early 1980s, Cardiff, starved of investment, was a classic case of a city in decline, but twenty years later, the city is held up as a model of urban renaissance. The two catalysts for this remarkable turnaround were the redevelopment of the Cardiff Bay and the construction of Millennium Stadium.[11] The economic impact of the Millennium Stadium, which was expressly built for the 1999 Rugby World Cup, has been immense and has prompted additional investment in the city's infrastructure, with improvements to rail transport and to access and circulation at the Central Railway Station and Central Square. The stadium also inspired environmental improvements along the River Taff, and the County Council funded the Stadium River Walk.

The Cardiff experience was relevant to the situation faced by

"A clear trend in large sports developments around the world is the shared vision that sport and entertainment should be an essential part of the community. The infrastructure of our cities, whether existing or proposed, should be designed to allow the venues to be a part of everyday life. Stadia are, truly, buildings that can support a 24/7 approach to city life."

the famous Arsenal football club in north London. The club's much-loved Highbury stadium was nearing the end of its life and the club required a much larger seating capacity. Faced with this need to build a new venue Arsenal looked at a number of sites elsewhere in London, but there was no real doubt that they would remain in the Islington area. The local council were unanimous in their desire to keep the club in the district, and a preferred site was finally identified at Ashburton Grove, near Highbury. The site covers 11 hectares (27 acres), and the new stadium is part of an integrated urban planning exercise, which will be one of the largest urban regeneration projects in the UK. The masterplan includes the building of 1000 'key-worker' houses for service industry employees, such as nurses, teachers and firemen, who are finding it increasingly difficult to afford accommodation in London. A district waste and recycling plant is incorporated in the plan, along with a community sports centre, healthcare facilities and children's nurseries. The Ashburton Grove project is intended to regenerate the Lower Holloway Road area, currently one of the poorest districts in London. The old stadium at Highbury will be transformed with a £60 million project, which includes converting the heritage-listed Art Deco grandstands into apartments.

9 A banner on Benfica's new stadium rising on the site of the old building in Lisbon reads, 'SEJA UM DOS FUNDORES DA NOVA CATEDRAL E FAÇA PARTE DE HISTÓRIA DO BENFICA'.
10 Jim Antoniou, "Traumatic transformations in Athens in preparation for the Olympics", Architectural Review, No.1287, London, May 2004.
11 The regeneration of Cardiff Bay has been achieved with £850 million of private investment and includes the new National Assembly for Wales. The Bay, with its 200 hectare waterbody created by the Cardiff Bay Barrage, is also the location of the new £86 million Millennium Centre, which is the Headquarters of the Welsh National Opera Company and other art groups. It has a 2,000 capacity main arena with several other smaller performance areas.

Above: Estádio da Luz – Lisbon, Portugal 2003

Above: Nanjing Sports Park – Nanjing, Peoples Republic of China 2005

"The 'Stadium City' tends to develop in one of two ways: it either creates a completely new town, as in Nanjing; or it fills the gaps in an existing city grid. A critical part of the planning of this new generation of stadia is the infrastructure grid. An essential question to be answered is whether a new grid should be created, or whether the existing grid can be modified and expanded to accommodate the demands of the new stadium. To be truly sustainable, the stadium needs to combine with other major new development. A core part of the philosophy must be that the stadium is not the end result, but part of a larger process where the focus is on community building."

In the ancient Chinese capital of Nanjing, the US$250 million Nanjing Sports Park is currently nearing completion. Located on the Yangtze riverfront, the centre includes a 60,000-seat stadium, an 11,000 capacity arena, an Olympic standard aquatic centre, baseball courts and 20 tennis courts. The Sports Park was the catalyst for the creation of an entire new city precinct to the west of Nanjing, known as the Hexi Second Downtown Precinct. The philosophy behind the development is that the new sports development will create a 'People's Place' for the city.

New Places of Public Assembly

Stadia are a vital component of new public space in the 21st Century, along with airport terminals, retail mega malls, multiplex cinemas and hypermarkets. Often they are privately owned spaces accommodating public functions. All these building types have the potential, often unrealised, to regenerate cities.

They are the 'new' places of public assembly. They complement, and to some extent have replaced, the cathedral square, the market place, the souk and the piazza. But all these new typologies are essentially inward looking: the public space is privatised and there has been no imperative to provide well-designed public space – attractive, seductive and inviting. The urban qualities of the areas in the immediate vicinity of many stadia have been remarkably disappointing. Surrounded by carparks, there has been no visible effort to improve the immediate environment, and security considerations and the policing of large crowds have often dominated the urban planning. The stadium typology can be anti-urban, as the venues are usually designed to be 'secure' and to exclude all those who do not have a legitimate reason to enter. Many American baseball parks make a positive contribution to the urban domain, as they fit into the existing grain of a city and create a human scale, but large football and multi-use stadia are more difficult to absorb into the urban fabric. A challenge to stadium designers is to improve urban design in the vicinity of stadia, and to implement the new generation of stadia, which must function as living parts of their cities.

Galpharm Stadium

(formerly Alfred McAlpine Stadium)

Huddersfield, England

1993

With its inventive use of subtly arched steel trusses supporting the roofs on all four sides of the pitch, the Huddersfield stadium heralded the beginning of a new era in British stadium design. The dramatic curved form of the stadium stands out in the grey and frequently overcast industrial landscape to the east of the Pennines. The distinctive roof-form provides a powerful identity for the Huddersfield soccer and rugby clubs, and symbolizes the resurgence of the Yorkshire mill town. The 24,700 capacity stadium fits comfortably into the contours of the banks of the Colne River, nestling against the slopes of the wooded Kilner Bank.

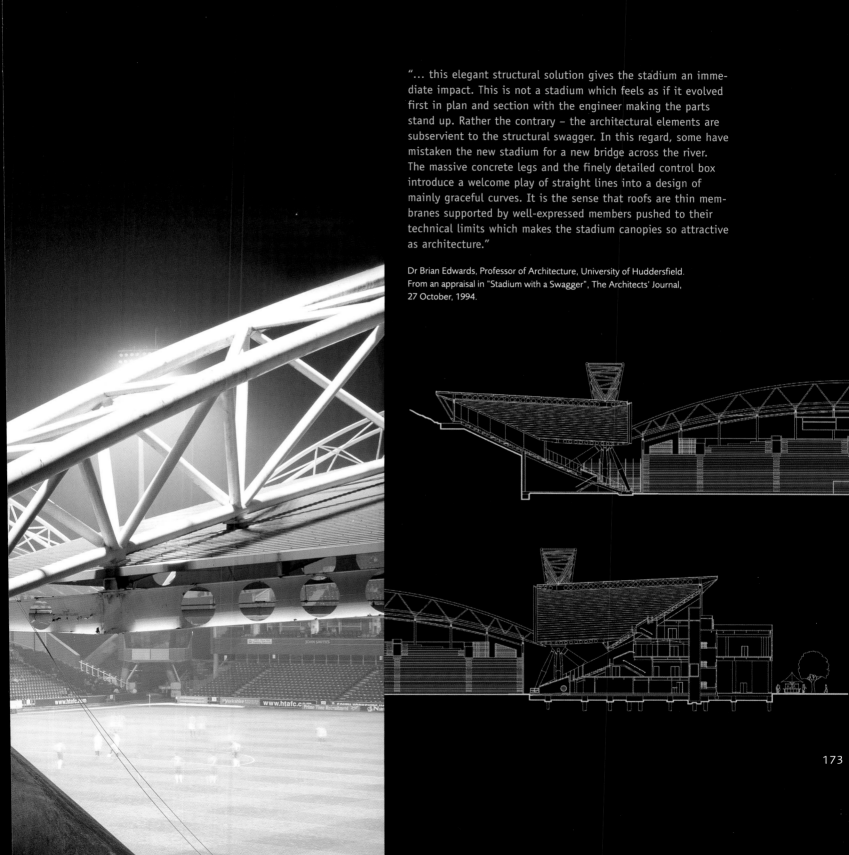

"... this elegant structural solution gives the stadium an immediate impact. This is not a stadium which feels as if it evolved first in plan and section with the engineer making the parts stand up. Rather the contrary – the architectural elements are subservient to the structural swagger. In this regard, some have mistaken the new stadium for a new bridge across the river. The massive concrete legs and the finely detailed control box introduce a welcome play of straight lines into a design of mainly graceful curves. It is the sense that roofs are thin membranes supported by well-expressed members pushed to their technical limits which makes the stadium canopies so attractive as architecture."

Dr Brian Edwards, Professor of Architecture, University of Huddersfield.
From an appraisal in "Stadium with a Swagger", The Architects' Journal, 27 October, 1994.

"Stadium design provides an almost unparalleled opportunity to combine architecture and engineering in close conjunction to a spectating audience. Rather than use deep lattice beams and cantilevers, which had become the pattern since the splendid 1930s design developed by the stadia architect Archibald Leach (for example Goodison Park, White Hart Lane, Craven Cottage), the design [for Huddersfield] has looked to oil rigs for inspiration. Tubular steel, bent into sweeping curves to produce prismatic trusses, proves surprisingly economic and has the necessary bold modern imagery. Though expensive in materials costs, the saving in weight, flexibility of use and ease of erection resulted in slight savings over conventional wide-span roofing systems. Just as the oil-rigs put design responsibility before material cost, so too this design is justified by pricing time, convenience and long-term adaptability."

Dr Brian Edwards, Professor of Architecture, University of Huddersfield. From an appraisal in "Stadium with a Swagger", The Architects' Journal, 27 October, 1994.

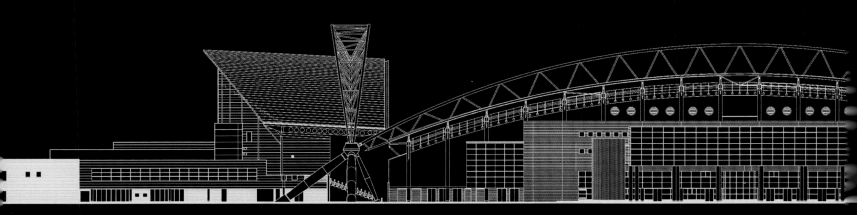

"From almost any angle of approach, the first glimpses are of weirdly white, skeletal arches looming above the rooftops of Huddersfield's weathered sandstone terraces or between its gas-ometers and chimneys. Do these incongruous white structures form part of a bridge, or perhaps a fairground ride?

Closer to, the whiteness of the arches comes sharply into focus against the trees on Kilner Bank, which rise up behind the stadium like a hazy, green backcloth.

But closer still and the stadium now cuts right into its sur-rounds. The familiar soft colours of a West Yorkshire townscape are now but faded pastels next to the shiny hard, metallic, almost clinical blues, yellows, reds and greys of the stands. Sapphire blue glazed bricks line the curved frontage of the main Lawrence Batley Stand, offset by yellow window details. Blue profile metal sheets hug the gentle contours of the roof, under which the vertical cladding is in plain, ribbed metal. If skies are grey the details seem cold and mechanical. Under the sun, they shine like American motorhomes.

Clearly, this is like no other stadium you have ever seen before. And yet, the more you look, the simpler it all begins to appear. So simple in fact that even an untrained eye can readily understand the structure and marvel at the sheer lightness and transparency of its design. Those dominant roof trusses, for example. Dubbed the 'banana' trusses, they are, in section, inverted triangles.

Each stand is shaped like an orange segment, and for good reason. Studies suggest that a majority of spectators prefer to watch closer to the centres of each touchline. It is also known that the optimum viewing distance for rugby and football is a 90m circle drawn from the centre of the pitch. Thus, to fit within this circle each stand assumes the shape of a slightly flattened semicircle."

Simon Inglis. From 'Football Grounds of Britain', Collins Willow Publishers, 1996

... this West Yorkshire town has acquired a spectacular new landmark built alongside the River Colne and near to the upgraded canal. The river corridor, a neglected industrial backwater, is being converted into a green corridor with the stadium as a major point of attraction. The popular image of Huddersfield as a town of satanic mills in the shadow of a massive ICI works has been skilfully sidestepped by Kirklees Council, whose choice of site for the new stadium and patronage of such bold design reflects a concern to move preconceptions from the industrial to the post-industrial era."

Dr Brian Edwards, Professor of Architecture, University of Huddersfield. From an appraisal in "Stadium with a Swagger", The Architects' Journal, 27 October, 1994.

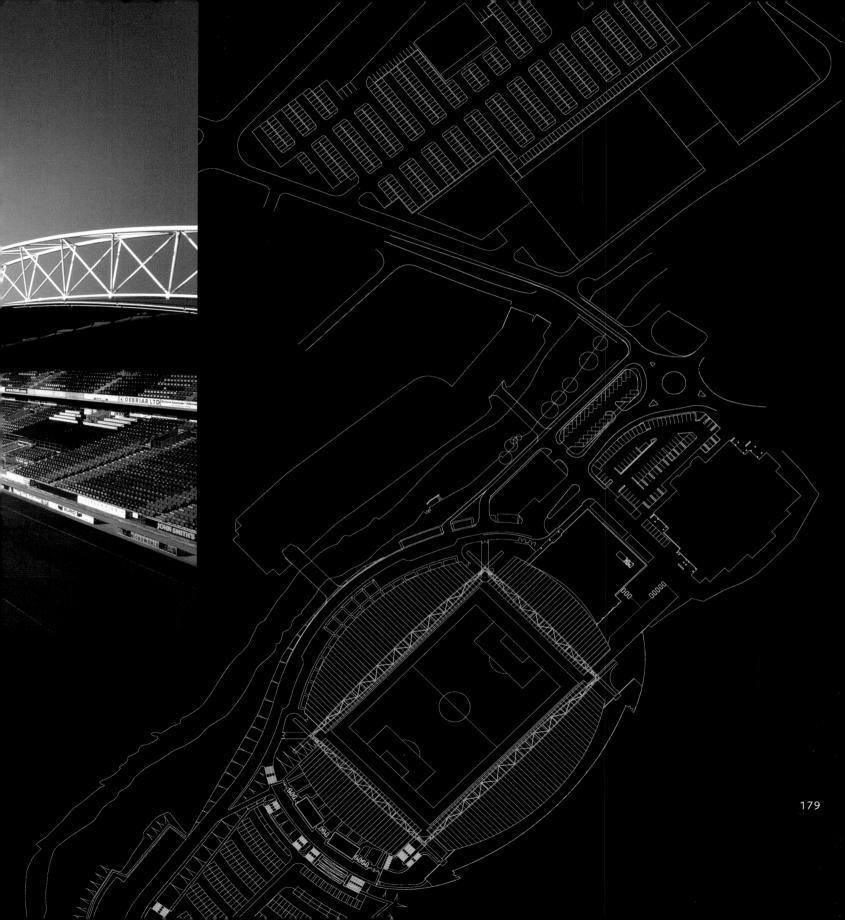

Nanjing Sports Park

Nanjing, Peoples Republic of China
2005

The Nanjing Sports Park forms the centrepiece of a new downtown precinct to the west of the city of Nanjing, an historic capital of China situated on the Yangtze River. The new development includes a 60,000 seat stadium, a 13,000 seat indoor sports arena, an Olympic standard aquatic centre, a tennis centre and outdoor facilities for hockey, baseball and basketball. Recreational park space takes up 35 percent of the complex, as part of a deliberate strategy to create a 'People's Place' for the city of Nanjing. The sports buildings are grouped closely together, and are accessed by an elevated podium which separates the sporting crowds from the surrounding parkland.

The role of this sporting complex in creating a new downtown for Nanjing is of great significance at the beginning of the 21st Century. There are many global examples of how sports facilities can revitalize a community, but the Nanjing Sports Park demonstrates a new way of thinking: one that proposes the use of the sporting complex to create an entire city, or a new city within a city.

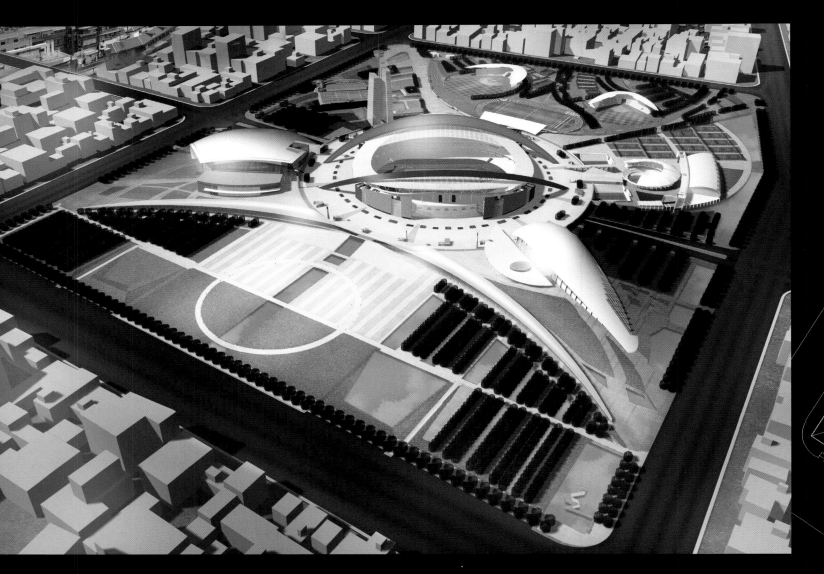

"The Nanjing Olympic Sports Centre is in the European style: free and romantic, like a garden. The design retains a style of natural flow and power, taking into account Chinese architectural theories and principles. The design stresses the main front view along Jinshi Road, its openness gives people a relaxed and happy prospect, and the main entrance is very formal and dignified. The master plan is a fine fusion of traditional symmetrical Chinese architecture with a relaxed and romantic Western style."

Nanjing Morning News, 26 March, 2002.

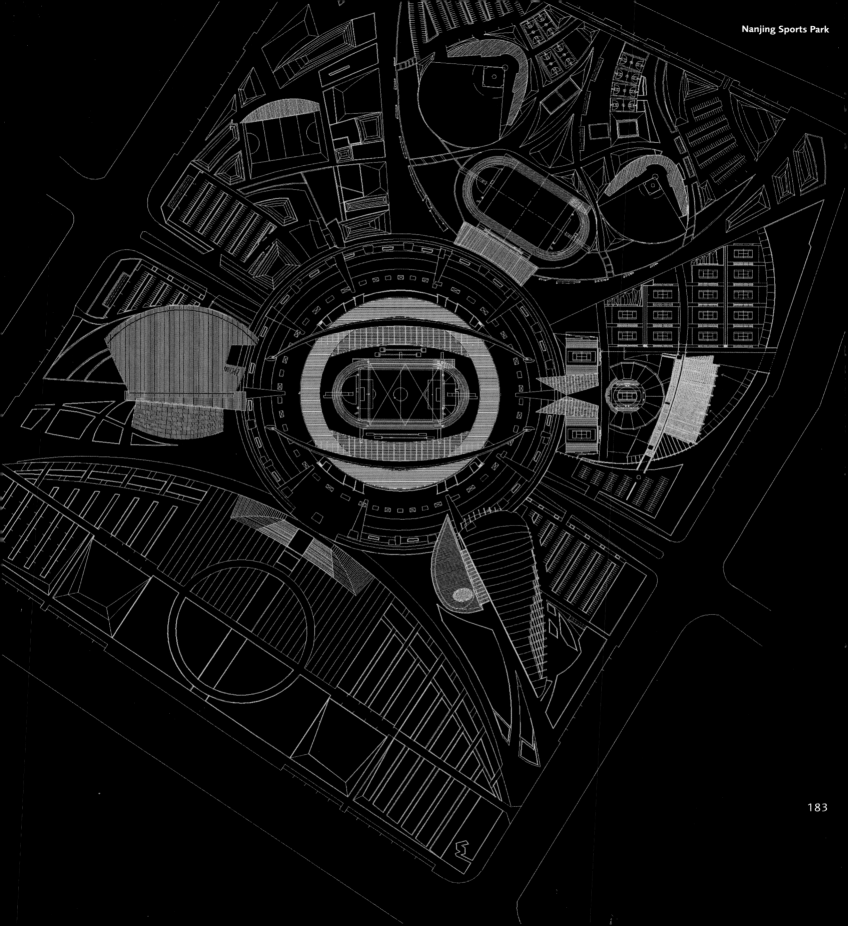

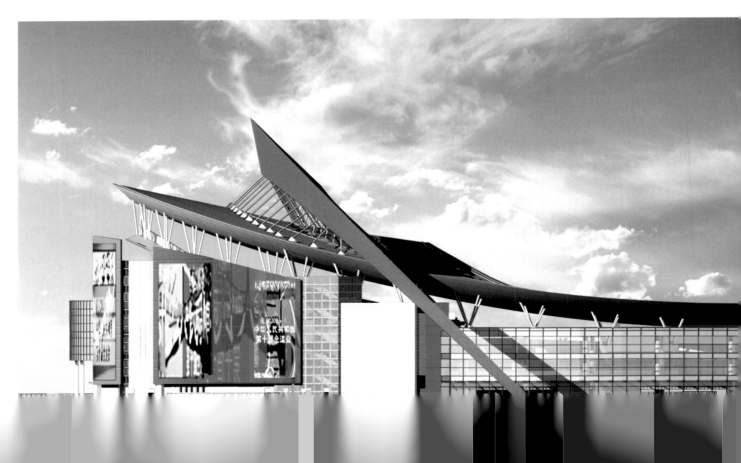

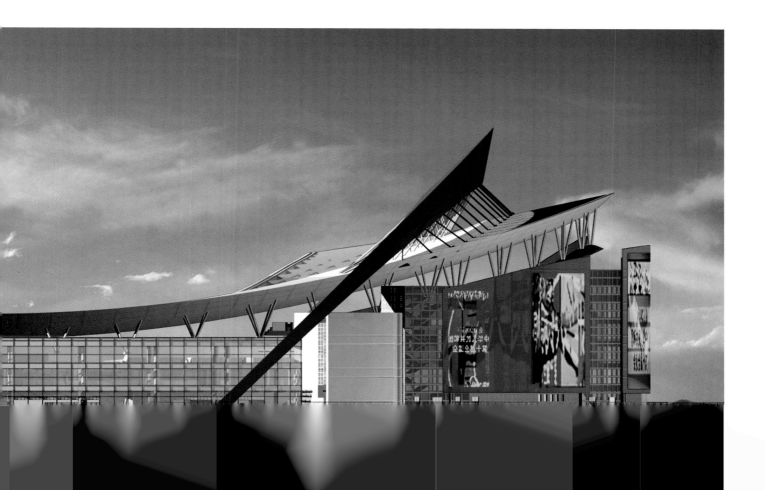

Emirates Stadium

London, England

2006 (scheduled completion)

Emirates Stadium, the new home of the Arsenal Football Club in north London, has been conceived as a focus for the community, located within an urban park with a public plaza around the perimeter. The 60,000 seat stadium will replace the much loved and revered Highbury stadium, which could only accommodate 38,000 spectators. The form of the stadium is a perfect ellipse with eight cores arranged symmetrically around the circumference, accommodating stairs and elevators. On top of the eight structural cores are steel tripods supporting the two primary trusses, which each measure 220 metres long by 15 metres high: the result is a clean-edged roofline and an uncluttered soffit. A five-metre high public podium encircles the stadium, and will be available for use by the local community on non-match days.

Emirates Stadium is part of an integrated urban planning exercise, one of Britain's largest urban regeneration projects, which will also see the construction of over 2,000 new homes and create over 1,800 new jobs in the Borough of Islington.

187

"I've enjoyed every minute that I've played at Highbury; it's a special place. But I think everyone knows that this great old stadium isn't sufficient for a club of Arsenal's ambitions. Certainly most games we play could be watched by thousands more who can't get tickets. Moving just down the road to a 60,000 capacity stadium seems the ideal solution to me."

- Dennis Bergkamp, from the Arsenal FC website.

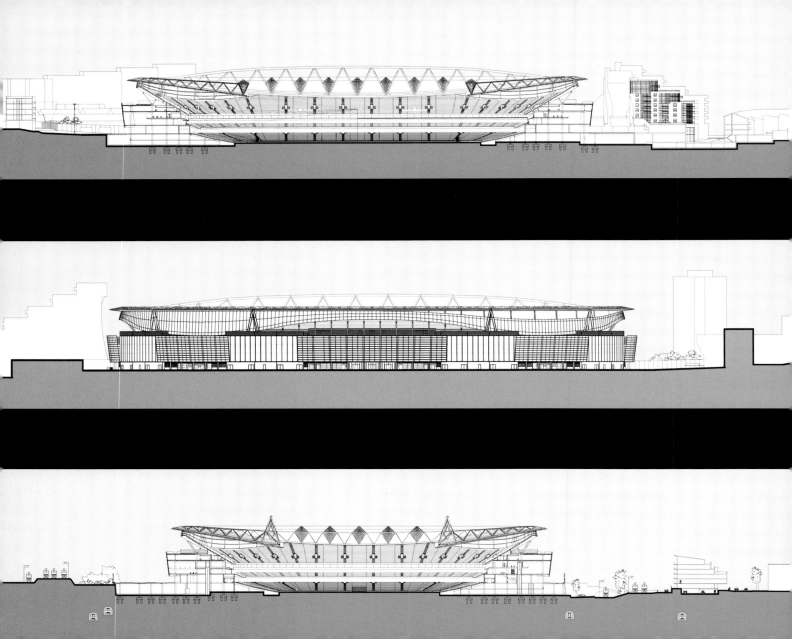

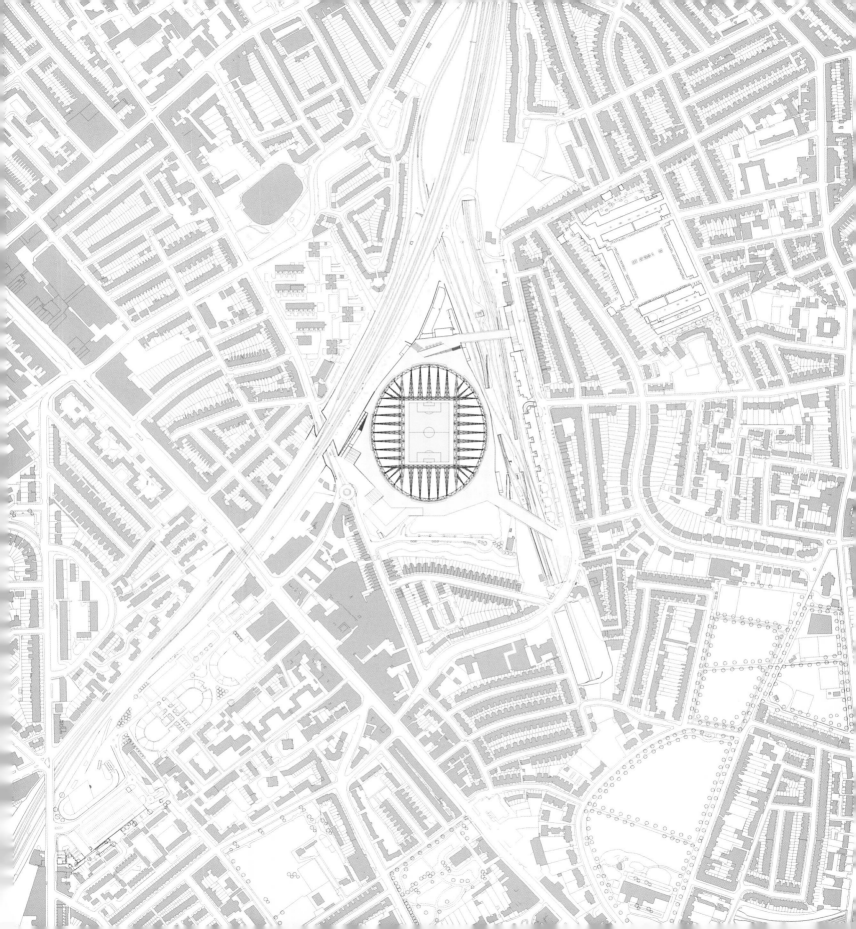

"Located halfway between Europe and Asia, Dubai is spending vast amounts of marketing money insinuating itself into our mental maps. In much the same way that the film industry made California the world's most desirable destination, Dubai is spending its capital on extraordinarily generous sponsorships. The costliest of these is the £100m that the city-state's airline, Emirates, spent naming Arsenal's new stadium (the biggest club deal in football history). For the next 15 years at least, the name Emirates Stadium will ring out across the UK, further spreading the word about the little sheikdom that talks big and acts audaciously."

Leonard Doyle. From "Arabian Heights", The Independent, 20 November, 2004.

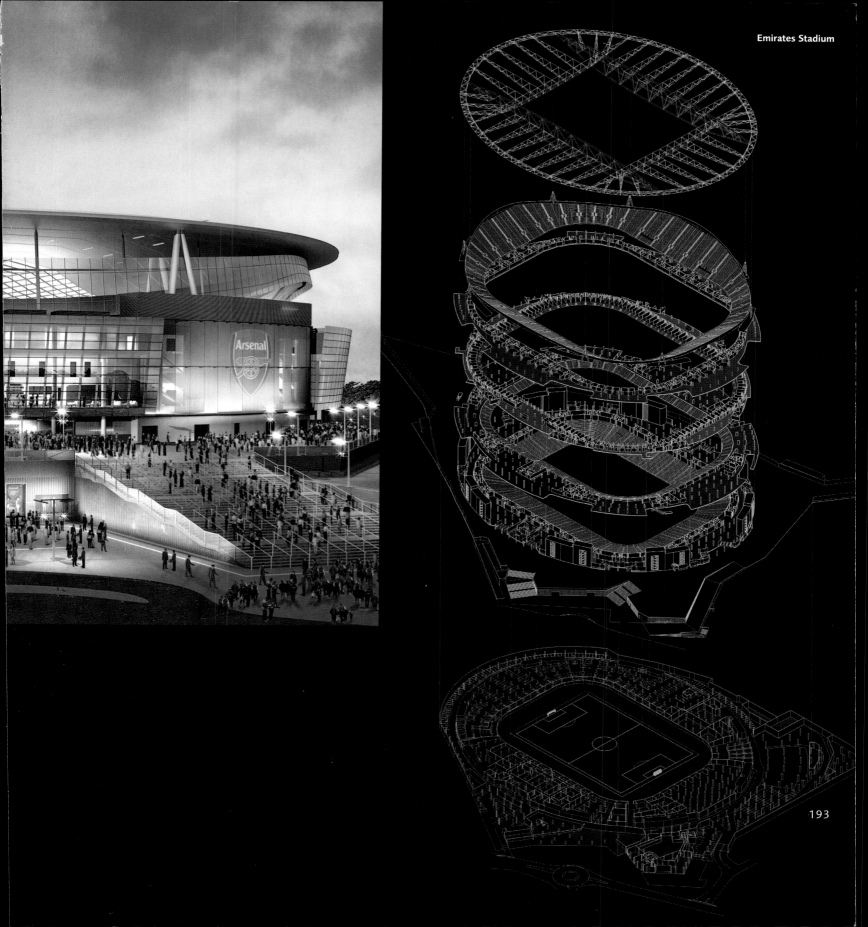

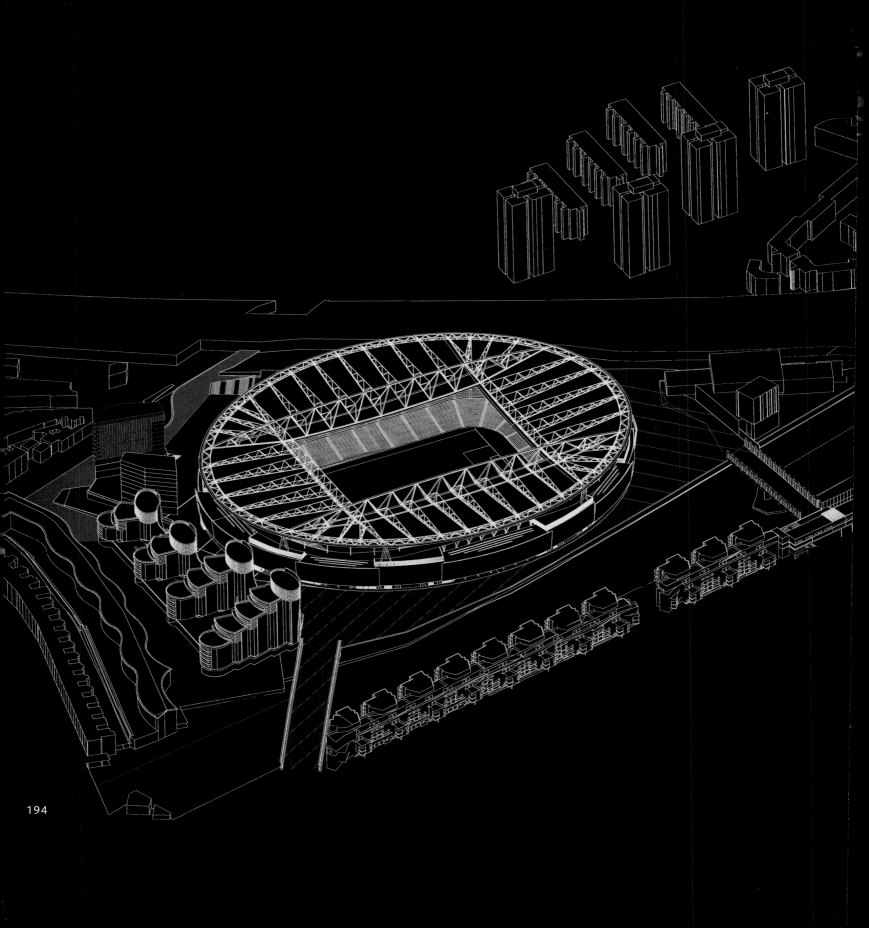

Telstra Stadium

(formerly Stadium Australia)

Sydney, Australia

1999

"The design of Stadium Australia [now Telstra Stadium] aimed at excellence on three levels.

Firstly as a focus of international recognition during the millennial Olympics: the stadium must have immediate recognition ability, unifying people's mental image of the Olympics and linking those images firmly with the city of Sydney.

Secondly as a functional sports facility: the pitch, the stands and the support facilities must offer maximum pleasure to players and spectators, drawing happy crowds and motivating athletes to set world records.

Thirdly as a valued part of the sporting and cultural life of Sydney and Australia for decades to come: this requires built-in durability, adaptability and design with long-term power as an icon in the Sydney landscape, taking its place alongside the internationally recognized Harbour Bridge and the Opera House."

Rod Sheard.

Telstra Stadium, formerly Stadium Australia, was designed by an HOK Sport + Venue + Event joint venture, Bligh Lobb Sports Architecture.

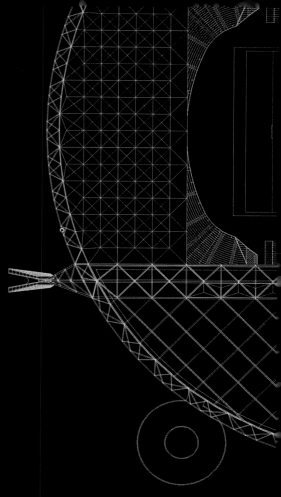

"Stadium Australia is large enough to accommodate the greatest of sporting spectacles: flexible to ensure its ongoing viability through continuous use, and mindful of the level of amenity and accessibility required to draw spectators out of the comfort of television viewing and into the moment when athletes and spectators are bonded, each driving the other, to create sport's sublime moments."

Harry Margalit. From "Stadium Australia" in 'Olympic Architecture; Building Sydney 2000' by Patrick Bingham-Hall. Watermark Press, Sydney, 1999.

Following the 2000 Olympic Games, the terraced seating at the north and south ends of the stadium was removed, reducing capacity from 110,000 to 80,000. The athletics track was torn up and the stadium was reconfigured with a rectangular pitch (opposite above) to suit rugby league, rugby union and soccer. Seating on both sides of the stadium was moved closer to the playing surface, and the roof was completed to create a perfect circular form, dipping at the north and south end of the amphitheatre. The stadium can also be converted to an oval shape (opposite below) for cricket and Australian Rules football.

The vista from the upper level of Telstra Stadium is mind-blowing. The eye is drawn to the flowing curve of the stadium roof as it dips behind the goal posts before sweeping dramatically upwards at the centre line: one's gaze then drops far below the encompassing rows of seats to the field of play. The emotional experience of the stadium is breathtaking – not unlike the first time that one enters the Campo in Siena.

Telstra Stadium is firmly in the tradition of Australian stadia as a multi-purpose venue, but it is the most technologically advanced Olympic Stadium ever built, and the roof is the most conspicuous design feature. The translucent saddle-shaped roof (which has been likened to an Aussie bushranger's hat) slopes down towards the pitch, thereby enhancing the intense atmosphere and optimising the stadium acoustics. This configuration also reduces glare and shadow on the field, ensuring ideal conditions for daytime TV broadcasts.

The roof covering of translucent polycarbonate tiles is separated by a series of stainless steel drainage gutters, and the entire structure is contained within a framework flexible enough to cope with the curves of the roof plane and the expansion of the polycarbonate in intense sunlight. The stadium is one of the few in the world that effectively shades and protects most spectators, without the need for a fully enclosed dome.

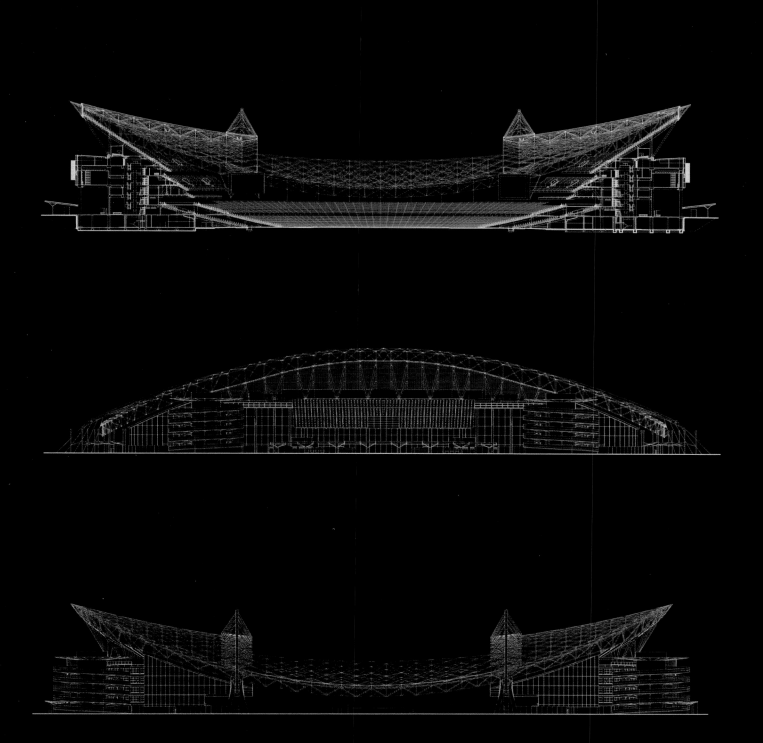

"Stadium Australia opened this summer, and it will be judged on more than just sightlines. An Olympic stadium is an architectural message to the world, an icon embodying the health and aspirations of a nation. Designers are fast catching on to the stadium's role as a cultural and commercial flagship, and as the US hands the baton of innovation to Europe and Asia, the market for the world's most watched building type is hotter than ever."

World Architecture magazine, October 1999

"I am proud and happy to proclaim that you have presented to the world the best Olympic Games ever."

Juan Antonio Samaranch, President of the IOC, at the closing ceremony of the 2000 Olympic Games in Stadium Australia (now Telstra Stadium).

Acknowledgments

All photography © by Patrick Bingham-Hall
except as listed below:

Thorney Lieberman © p36; 160
Mark Green © p62
Assassi © p63
Timothy Hursley © p66; 67
Jeff Goldberg/ESTO Photographics © p85; 86; 87; 158
From the archives of The Daily Mail, London © p102
Gerry Cranham/Transworld © p108
Joel Avila/Hawkeye Aerial Photography © p132
David Simmonds © p139
Jim Schafer © p162

Computer images courtesy HOK Sport © p24; 77; 168; 181; 182; 184
Computer image courtesy MCG5 Architects © p17
Computer images courtesy GMJ for WNSL © p24; 31
Computer images courtesy WST © p29; 30
Computer images courtesy Studio Blue © p69; 70; 73
Computer images courtesy Miller Hare © p 186; 189; 192; 195
Gustav Klutsis reproduction courtesy State Museum of Riga, Latvia © p105

208